OVERCOMING
ANXIETY,
WORRY,
AND
FEAR

Books by Gregory L. Jantz, PhD, with Ann McMurray

Healing the Scars of Emotional Abuse
How to De-Stress Your Life
Every Woman's Guide to Managing Your Anger

OVERCOMING
ANXIETY,
WORRY,
AND
FEAR

Practical Ways to Find Peace

GREGORY L. JANTZ, PhD,

WITH ANN MCMURRAY

Revell

a division of Baker Publishing Group
Grand Rapids, Michigan

© 2011 by Gregory L. Jantz

Published by Revell
a division of Baker Publishing Group
P.O. Box 6287, Grand Rapids, MI 49516-6287
www.revellbooks.com

Printed in the United States of America

Library of Congress Cataloging-in-Publication Data
Jantz, Gregory L.
    Overcoming anxiety, worry, and fear : practical ways to find peace /
Gregory L. Jantz, with Ann McMurray.
        p.   cm.
    Includes bibliographical references.
    ISBN 978-0-8007-1968-5 (pbk.)
    1. Peace of mind—Religious aspects—Christianity. 2. Anxiety—Religious aspects—Christianity. 3. Worry—Religious aspects—Christianity. 4. Fear—Religious aspects—Christianity. I. McMurray, Ann. II. Title. III. Title: Practical ways to find peace.
    BV4908.5.J36 2011
    248.8′6—dc22   2011006155

The names of persons who have come to the Center for counseling have been changed, and some illustrations are a combination of individual stories to protect confidentiality.

In keeping with biblical principles of creation stewardship, Baker Publishing Group advocates the responsible use of our natural resources. As a member of the Green Press Initiative, our company uses recycled paper when possible. The text paper of this book is composed in part of post-consumer waste.

11   12   13   14   15   16   17   7   6   5   4   3   2   1

This book is dedicated to all those imprisoned by the burden
of their own anxieties, worries, and fears
yet determined to experience freedom, peace, and joy again.
There is hope!

Contents

Contents

Introduction

One More Thing to Worry About

Do you ever find yourself fearful without really knowing why?

Do you worry about a thousand little things during the day?

Do certain situations cause your heart to race and your palms to sweat?

Do you sometimes feel like you're smothering, like you can't get enough air?

Do you all of a sudden feel light-headed, disconnected, and on edge?

Do you wake up in the morning tired and irritable?

Do you have trouble going to sleep or staying asleep?

Does the fear sometimes become so overwhelming that you're afraid you're going to die?

Do you avoid certain people, places, and situations because of how fearful they make you feel?

Do you find yourself thinking about all the things that could go wrong?

In an age of the twenty-four-hour news cycle, instant messaging, and Amber Alerts, terrorist attacks, health epidemics, and natural disasters, environmental toxins, economic collapses, and diseases of the month, we have a lot to be worried about. It seems the more we know, the more we worry. It seems the sooner we know, the longer we have to worry. We worry about our world, our community, our family. In this age of unemployment, layoffs, downsizing, and corporate mergers, we worry about our careers, our jobs, and our livelihood. In this permissive society, we worry about our marriages and our relationships. We grow concerned as we age about our looks and our health. With growing obesity, we worry about our weight. On and on it goes. For some of us, we never seem to jettison a current worry before we take on another. The accumulated burden of so much worry begins to take an emotional, relational, physical, and spiritual toll. All this worrying makes us anxious. What will we do? How will we cope? What's it all going to mean?

Anxiety is defined as "a painful or apprehensive uneasiness of the mind, usually over an impending or anticipated ill; a fearful concern or interest; an abnormal or overwhelming sense of apprehension and fear often marked by physiological signs (as sweating, tension, and increased pulse), by doubt concerning the reality and nature of the threat, and by self-doubt about one's capacity to cope with it."[1] Too many of us live out this definition in our lives. The opposite of worry and anxiety—assurance, calm, composure, confidence, contentment, ease, happiness, peace, security, tranquility—is foreign. We'd love to go there; we just don't know the way.

If you're like me, sometimes you just aren't able to put your fears into perspective or set your concerns aside. That's normal; some things take longer to work through than others. However, what do you do when these worries and fears build day after day, leading to a state of anxiety? What do you do when every day you feel like you're gearing up for a battle but you don't know when the first blow will strike? As Christians, it doesn't help to read in

Scripture that we're supposed to "be anxious about nothing" when it seems we're anxious about *everything*.

Over my years in the counseling business, I've seen the toll anxiety takes on lives and health. I've seen anxiety partner with many other mental health, medical, and chemical dependency concerns, complicating recovery. I've seen fear of the future outweigh the horror of the present, resulting in paralysis and an inability to move forward.

I've also seen people meet their worries, fear, and anxieties head-on, helping them break through to recovery. I've seen the amazing courage of those who refused to cower any longer in a corner of their lives and reached out and up to personal victory. I've seen hope win out over despair, trust win out over fear, faith triumph over adversity. I've seen people win and gain back their lives.

If you feel like you've been defeated by anxiety and fear, I want you to win and gain back your life. This book will help you look at the reasons behind excessive worry and anxiety in your life, reaching back to the fears at the root. With assurances from God's Word and practical, everyday alternatives, this book will present valuable insights to help you stop the runaway train of anxiety and panic. You'll learn how to bring order and calm into life's daily challenges instead of being run over by them. You'll learn practical information on how to unchain yourself from self-doubt, fear, and constant worry. Presented from a whole-person point of view, this book will outline the emotional, relational, physical, and spiritual factors involved with persistent worry, as well as avenues for positive change.

Anxiety and worry tend to cause reality to become unhinged, spiraling farther and farther away from the truth. So at the end of each chapter, you'll find an anchoring activity. Each one is designed to help bring you back to earth, to help you become more grounded in truth and reality.

Would you like to experience peace in your life—a peace you could count on?

Would you like to be able to face your fears and come out the winner?

Would you like to understand what all this fear and worry you feel is about?

Would you like to know how to overcome the panic and really enjoy life again?

Would you like to look forward to the future instead of creeping up on it with dread?

You weren't created to live a life of worry, with fears and anxieties constantly hedging you in and draining you of happiness, joy, and peace. It's time to step back from the edge and overcome your anxiety, worry, and fear.

PART 1

Understanding the Effect of Anxiety, Worry, and Fear

1

Is It Just Me?

Anxiety Disorders, Panic Attacks, and Phobias

Some people are just natural worriers. Worry is their default setting for life. Some people's worry comes in the neon colors of hysteria. They're called high-strung, tense, edgy. They're called frantic, overwrought, nervous. Others appear to wear the duller tones of their worry as comfortably as another person might a favorite sweater. They're called pessimists, worrywarts, moody. They're called critical, sometimes thoughtful, but always negative. Still others hide their fear, pushing it so far into the background of their lives that it's difficult to recognize. If they're called anything at all, it's depressed, resigned, or apathetic.

So many people worry about so many things in so many ways. When is it just someone's personality? When is a fear justified? When is anxiety way out of proportion? Is it just you? Just how prevalent is worry? According to the National Institutes of Health, almost forty million American adults suffer from an anxiety disorder.[1] An anxiety disorder isn't a temporary concern over a stressful situation, like meeting your future in-laws for the first time or making a presentation at work. Anxiety disorders show themselves by a couple of characteristics: they don't go away, and, left untreated, they get progressively worse.

Just as people are unique, with different characteristics, so are anxiety disorders. There are five identified anxiety disorders, and we'll go through each one:

1. generalized anxiety disorder (also known as GAD)
2. panic attacks
3. phobias, including social phobia or social anxiety disorder
4. obsessive-compulsive disorder (also known as OCD)
5. post-traumatic stress disorder (also known as PTSD)

One of the effects of an anxiety disorder is a sense of isolation. Sometimes people think they're going crazy, lost in a bizarre world where none of the pieces seem to fit right, resulting in a constant grinding and tension to life. For many people who suffer from anxiety, there is a sense of humiliation, a conviction that others will negatively judge either their inability to cope or the convoluted coping strategies they've devised merely to get through each day.

While each person uniquely experiences anxiety, fear, and worry, it is powerful when people can see themselves as not alone, understanding that others share a similar, if not identical, experience. So as you read these descriptions of the five types of anxiety disorders, realize you're looking for patterns, not a perfect alignment with every personal episode, encounter, or event.

Generalized Anxiety Disorder (GAD)

There's a reason why this anxiety disorder is characterized by the word *generalized*. In short, people with GAD worry about everything in general.

With a start, Mike realized he'd almost missed getting off at his stop. He'd been going over in his mind everything he'd done the day before to find the discrepancy on the latest production report. His supervisor told him it wasn't a big deal, but Mike still felt it was. Was this some sort of performance test? Were the higher-ups waiting to see how he'd respond and what he'd do to fix it? Did they think he was responsible? Or was he making too much out of it? Mike just didn't know, and not knowing meant it was all he could think about.

Mike had taken this route for almost six years to and from work, and yet here he was, yanking the cord at the last possible second. The bus driver probably thought he was an idiot for zoning out on his stop. As he hurriedly got off the bus, trying not to make eye contact, Mike wished he hadn't eaten such a big breakfast. His stomach was tied up in knots. What if he couldn't fix the problem? How much time could he devote to finding the answer and not have other tasks lapse? Who was watching and how closely? It was a tough economy, and Mike was relieved to have his job, which meant he was terrified of losing it.

Suddenly, his heart began to race. His increased breathing had nothing to do with the slight incline he climbed toward the back entrance to work. It *was* a tough economy. What would he do if he lost his job? By the time Mike had plastered on the semblance of a smile as he clocked in, he'd already imagined the domino effect of losing his job, house, esteem of his wife, respect of his kids, and the fragile reputation with his friends. With the thoughts of potential disaster swirling in his mind, he knew it would be difficult to concentrate at work today, but he'd have to find a way. The only avenue to avoid potential calamity was eternal vigilance. He had to be on his guard at all times. With a sigh, Mike twisted his neck from side to side, wishing he'd been able to get more sleep last night. It was going to be a long day.

If this was the first and only time Mike had experienced this kind of episode, you could write it off to a temporary problem at work; it wouldn't indicate GAD. However, if this scene is replayed day after day, just with different problems, anxieties, conflicts, and concerns, it is GAD. GAD isn't a single bad day or even a bad week; it's an ongoing state of worry, concern, and heightened anxiety over everyday events for six months or more. It's constant worry about *what if, what might, what could* with no discernible solution, no end, and no peace.

This incessant state of pending catastrophe leaves a person awash in the toxicity of their own stress. It's not healthy. With no off switch, the mind and body are kept at a heightened state of alert, which takes a physical and emotional toll. According to the National Institutes of Health, many people with GAD know they worry too much; they just can't seem to control their thoughts. They worry about everyday things every day. This constant worrying leaves them easily startled. They have trouble falling or staying asleep and find it almost impossible to relax for any length of time. With so many things to worry about, they have a hard time concentrating.

Here are some of the other common symptoms of GAD:

- feeling tired for no reason
- headaches
- muscle tension and aches
- having a hard time swallowing
- trembling or twitching
- being irritable
- sweating
- nausea
- feeling light-headed
- feeling out of breath
- having to go to the bathroom frequently
- hot flashes[2]

Often, I'm not the first professional someone suffering from GAD goes to for help. She or he (I put "she" first because GAD affects twice as many women as men)[3] will first go to a physician for relief from one or more of the physical symptoms. Depending on the circumstances, it can take numerous visits to rule out purely physical reasons for the symptoms.

One woman I worked with came to me after repeated visits to her primary care physician. She went to him originally because she was convinced she had some sort of breathing disorder or lung dysfunction. Simply put, she was having trouble breathing and swallowing. After a series of examinations and tests, her doctor told her there was nothing structurally wrong with her esophagus or lungs. Instead, the overwhelming anxiety she chronically experienced was causing her to constrict the muscles in her throat. She was, quite literally, asphyxiating herself because of the stress of her worry. Her doctor told her it was endangering her life and put her on medication. He also told her she needed the help of a mental health specialist.

Generalized anxiety disorder is serious. It has long-term debilitating effects. It consumes time, energy, and relationships. It leaches joy, contentment, and peace from your life.

Panic Attacks

If generalized anxiety disorder can be compared to a low-level, persistent, white-noise worry, a panic attack is a sonic boom of terror. Exploding at any time for no discernible reason, a panic attack feels like a life-threatening event.

Angela talked about a panic attack like someone would a stalker. She never knew when it would strike or over what circumstance—real or imagined. It could hit almost anywhere, when she was in the midst of a crowd of people or alone in her apartment. Suddenly, something inside would change. Her body would respond to the panic overtaking her before her mind could register the shift. It was as if she became unhinged from the present, tethered instead to the formless panic dragging her into a smothering abyss. Her breathing sped as her heart raced, so loud she was sure it must be ready to burst out of her chest. The first time it happened, on her way home from a sales meeting, she was convinced she was having a heart attack. Half a night at the emergency room had proven otherwise. She'd been told her heart was fine. Her life wasn't because the panic attacks continued.

They were so overwhelming and severe that Angela was terrified of them. She lived with a sense of impending ambush. Because she couldn't seem to control them once they hit, Angela decided to avoid situations where she'd had one. That was why she never went to a movie theater anymore. That time, when the panic struck in the darkened theater, she was able to pass it off as a sudden illness, afraid her companion would think she was crazy. Now, she had to wait for movies to come out on DVD. Of course, she no longer allowed herself to see any sort of action movie, even at home, for fear of triggering an attack.

The worst times, though, were at night. She'd had so many panic attacks in the quiet of her bedroom that she'd lost count. Angela dreaded going to bed. Each night was a struggle between the panic she feared and the rest she needed. Lately, because of her constant exhaustion, she knew she was losing the battle.

Primary care physicians are often the first health-care professionals to see someone with GAD. For those with panic attacks, the first line of defense is often the emergency room. The symptoms of a panic attack are not "in your head." They are real, physical, and immediate. They are so real that people in the midst of a panic attack describe it, like Angela, as a heart attack. Others experience it as a crippling fear of imminent death. The physical response to this fear is extreme:

- pounding heart—this isn't just an irregular or rapid heart-beat but can also be a sense that your heart is jumping out of your chest because it's beating so hard

- sweatiness
- dizziness, vertigo, or feeling faint
- trembling or shaking
- nausea or upset stomach
- feeling either flushed and hot or chilled and cold
- tingling hands and feet or numbness
- a feeling of not being able to get enough air, of suffocating
- pain or tightness in the chest

According to the National Institutes of Health, panic attacks tend to begin in late adolescence and early adulthood. Like GAD, women appear to be affected by panic attacks twice as often as men.[4] These are not subtle events; they are more like getting hit broadside. They are, however, relatively short-lived, with the bulk of the symptoms lasting around ten minutes.[5] Those ten minutes, though, can seem like a lifetime if you're the one suffering through them. And while the panic attack itself may do its worst for only about ten minutes, the fear and anxiety over when the next one will strike can be persistent and ongoing.

Phobias

GAD is scattershot anxiety—extraordinary worry over ordinary things. Panic attacks are a stealth strike of fear—extraordinary terror over nothing discernible. Phobias combine the elements of ordinary things and extraordinary terror. When I looked on Wikipedia, I found almost one hundred types of phobias listed, including a section devoted to fictional ones. For those with specific phobias, the fear and terror are anything but fictional; they are very real.

When Jillian's new co-worker asked if she wanted to ride with her after work to the retirement party, Jillian hesitated. She didn't want to seem rude, but she didn't know what kind of car her co-worker drove. Jillian also wanted to leave a little bit early so she could be one of the first to the restaurant in order to pick out her seat. It wasn't that she was antisocial; Jillian was claustrophobic. It was impossible for her to ride in a small car, and she was incapable of sitting at the back of a large booth, wedged in by other people.

At work, Jillian never took the elevator to the fourth floor; she always used the stairs. Even the stairwell was a little restricted, but it was infinitely better than the enclosed box of the elevator. When her division had moved onto that floor two years ago, Jillian had volunteered for the noisier, more centrally located cubicle because it was larger than the more private and quieter options farther down the hall. The others thought she was being unselfish. She'd laughed inside at that. She had been *extremely* selfish and would have put up a fight with anyone who'd tried to claim her refuge. Being enclosed was simply not an option for Jillian. Every new situation had to be factored through that filter.

Jillian gave her co-worker the excuse that she wanted to leave early to pick up a card on the way. The explanation worked without causing a problem. Now, if the rest of the evening could only go as smoothly.

Claustrophobia is one of the most common phobias. Here are some of the others:

- acrophobia—fear of heights
- agoraphobia—fear of crowds, open areas, or public spaces (literally fear of the marketplace)
- arachnophobia—fear of spiders
- aquaphobia—fear of water
- aviophobia—fear of flying
- bacillophobia—fear of germs
- cynophobia—fear of dogs
- hemophobia—fear of blood

- necrophobia—fear of death
- ophidiophobia—fear of snakes
- nomophobia—fear of being alone
- xenophobia—fear of strangers

Here are some obscure ones:

- coulrophobia—fear of clowns
- gephyrophobia—fear of crossing bridges
- heliophobia—fear of sunlight
- olfactophobia—fear of smells
- paraskavedekatriaphobia—fear of Friday the 13th

As strange as some of Wikipedia's nearly one hundred phobias are, they are really no laughing matter. Exposure to the object of a specific phobia can trigger a severe anxiety reaction or even a panic attack.

Some phobias can become tightly intertwined with panic attacks. Panic attack sufferers tend to avoid situations that triggered an attack in the past. Therefore, after each panic attack, their world shrinks. If they were at a restaurant and had an attack, they'll avoid going out to eat. If they are afraid of dogs, they may avoid taking walks in their own neighborhood. They'll avoid flying if they experienced a panic attack while boarding or on an airplane. If they suffered an attack driving down a specific street, they'll avoid traveling that same route, if not driving altogether. As their world shrinks, no place seems safe. This is the world of agoraphobia, where sufferers become incapable of leaving the perceived safety, security, and control of their own homes, sometimes even specific rooms within that home.

Once again, women appear to be twice as susceptible as men to phobias.[6] Childhood can be the beginning of a phobia that lasts through adolescence and persists into adulthood. Many people have found creative ways to work around their phobias, like Jillian. It's easier, of course, the more specific the phobia, like avoiding snakes or clowns. For other phobias, such as a fear of sunlight or water, avoidance has a greater impact on daily functioning. One of the phobias that has the most impact is social phobia, also known as social anxiety disorder.

Social phobia isn't just a fear of being around people. It's not a claustrophobic reaction to large crowds. This is a fear of being hurt by people in social settings, of being watched and judged by others. This is the extreme fear of being embarrassed under the harsh glare of others.

Over and over again, Greg berated himself for his cowardice. After all, it was just a harmless party. Granted, it was a harmless party he never should have agreed to attend, but he'd been boxed into going by his roommate, who found himself having to work unexpectedly. Realizing he was now going by himself caused Greg to break out in a fresh sweat. Perfect. He'd be drenched and stinky by the time he showed up.

Greg had been unable to come up with a good reason not to go, so he was stuck. Gritting his teeth, he promised himself he'd go, spend the shortest possible amount of time there, stand off in a corner hiding behind a drink, and take note of who else was there so he could report back to his roommate. Then, as soon as humanly possible, he'd sneak off to freedom.

As Greg got out of his car and walked toward the front door, he wiped his hands nervously on his pant legs. This sweating was ridiculous. Good thing it was cold outside; hopefully it wouldn't be too hot inside. All he needed was to broil in the sauna of his own sweat and discomfort. Looking left and right along the street, he felt relieved that he didn't recognize any other car. The fewer people he knew, the sooner he could leave. He'd already spent over a week worrying about this party, desperate to get out of it but fearful of annoying his roommate. The potential for disaster became more pressing the closer he got to the door. His total objective for the evening was to hide in plain sight and get out as soon as possible.

For those with social anxiety disorder, other people represent an enemy. People are adversaries just waiting for that one situation to criticize, belittle, judge, or publicly humiliate them. People are unsafe. The range of social phobia runs the gamut—from those who feel safe only with trusted family members, to those who experience anxiety around people only in specific situations, such as eating in front of others or speaking in public.

Unlike the other disorders mentioned so far, social anxiety disorder seems to affect men and women equally.[7] It appears to begin in childhood and continue on into the adult years. Social anxiety disorder, like panic attacks, can lead to agoraphobia, as the person creates a bunker mentality with home and family and is reluctant to venture out into a hostile world full of precarious situations ready to turn out badly and full of people ready to take advantage.

Those with social anxiety disorder experience the usual stress reactions of sweating, nausea, racing heart, and trembling. They may blush easily and have difficulty carrying on conversations. Unfortunately, these very symptoms can prove to be a barrier to effective communication and interaction. Not understanding the reasons, others can react to these symptoms by becoming hesitant, distrustful, and even dismissive of the person with the anxiety. Of course, this reaction merely fuels the anxiety.

Obsessive-Compulsive Disorder (OCD)

OCD is a harsh taskmaster. People who suffer from it live with an endless bombardment of obsessive thoughts. These thoughts are not positive or uplifting; they are filled with dread and sometimes are simply dreadful—imagining the death of a loved one or visualizing an act that is violent, sexual, and always personally repugnant. OCD is thought-life under siege. To cope with these despised intruders, OCD sufferers use specific actions to mitigate, manage, or control their thoughts. It's almost as if the actions are offered as a sacrifice in order to appease the thought tyrant. The actions become an imperative.

Trisha was late getting ready for work. Even though time was precious, she continued to count out the number of mascara strokes. Once she'd done ten on each set of lashes, she would wait another ten seconds for the mascara to dry and then complete the application by repeating it. Trisha did it the same way, every day, every time. It was the same with each of the things she did to get ready, from washing her hair to brushing her teeth. As long as she did it the same way every time, she knew she'd do it right. As long as she did it right, she was safe. As long as she did it right, her mother was safe.

Trisha lived in fear of doing something wrong, of not being what her mother called "presentable" whenever she went out in public. If she didn't get it right, her mother was going to die. She could see her mother's lifeless body in her mind, knowing she was responsible. To avoid this catastrophe, everything had to be done just right. Trisha chose certain types of clothes, with a minimum of buttons or zippers so she wouldn't have to spend so much time checking to make sure each button was fastened correctly or the zipper was zipped properly. This alone could set her back ten minutes or more, as she had to check multiple times for each—just to make sure. Failure was just too dreadful to contemplate, although she saw it in her mind all the time.

Just as Trisha was counting the number of times she'd brushed the lashes on her left side for the second time, the phone rang. She froze, torn between what might happen if she didn't answer the phone and what would happen if she did. By the third ring, she couldn't take the suspense any longer and ran to pick it up. After all, what if it was something important? What if it was her mother? What if she'd already done something wrong?

Breathless, she grabbed the phone. The voice on the other end asked Trisha if she had any donations to put out on the curb next Thursday. She tersely answered no and ended the call, realizing she was going to be even later to work than she'd planned. Everything was now ruined. She headed back to the shower, turned on the water, disrobed, and started her morning preparations all over again. Everything had to be done exactly the same way with no deviations, like answering telephones. It was the only way to keep the monsters at bay. It was the only way to keep from killing her mother.

OCD is all about keeping obsessive thoughts at bay with compulsive rituals. These thoughts can be comprised of unwanted images or impulses, often personally or religiously upsetting or repugnant. Because they are so upsetting or repugnant, great desperation is involved in trying to control them.

The rituals used often have to do with checking things over and over again, counting or physically touching items in a particular sequence. It is not just what the ritual entails that is important but the ritual itself. The preoccupation with the ritual helps mask the obsessive thought as well as act as an appeasement so the dreaded thought or image will not return.

Recently, the phenomenon known as hoarding has come into greater public awareness, propelled by graphic scenes on television showing homes crammed floor to ceiling with an astonishing amount of stuff. Shocking visuals show safety personnel in hazmat suits scooping out all manner of refuse and garbage, while the distraught hoarder pleads that every last bit of it is necessary. At times a home is filled with so many pets that they have become unclean, uncared for, and often ill.

Hoarding is considered an offshoot of OCD, but, recently, this categorization is being reevaluated.[8] It is possible that some time in the future hoarding will become its own distinct category. In the meantime, it's very real, and I'm finding more and more people opening up about the difficulty hoarding presents in their lives.

Without exception, their hoarding activity is always accompanied by varying levels of anxiety.

Hoarding both relieves anxiety and produces it. The more hoarders accumulate, the more insulated they feel from the world and its dangers. Of course, the more they accumulate, the more isolated they become from the world, including family and friends. Even the thought of discarding or cleaning out hoarded items produces extreme feelings of panic and discomfort.

It can be difficult to determine whether you are a hoarder or just a pack rat, someone who just likes to hang on to things. The main determiner of whether a behavior is just a personal preference or a disorder usually has to do with whether or not, and how much, that behavior has begun to negatively impact daily functioning. Here are generally recognized symptoms of hoarding from the Mayo Clinic:

- cluttered living spaces
- inability to discard items
- keeping stacks of newspapers, magazines, or junk mail
- moving items from one pile to another without discarding anything
- acquiring unneeded or seemingly useless items, including trash
- difficulty managing daily activities, procrastinating, and trouble making decisions
- difficulty organizing items
- perfectionism
- excessive attachment to possessions and discomfort letting others touch or borrow possessions
- limited or no social interactions

When your world is awash in anxiety, worry, and fear, and when accumulating things becomes a way to deflect and manage those feelings, the stacks will keep getting bigger and bigger.

Post-Traumatic Stress Disorder (PTSD)

Imagine being involved in a terrifying incident where you were physically harmed or threatened. Then imagine reliving that awful memory over and over again, each time as fresh and horrific as when it happened. This is the essence of PTSD.

Carrie was standing on the corner, waiting for her friend to pick her up. She still didn't feel safe driving, and Joel had been so good about getting her back and forth to work over the last several weeks. One minute, she was standing in the sunshine, waiting for Joel, and the next minute the sunshine had vanished. The corner had vanished. Carrie found herself right back at the scene of the accident. She could feel the blood dripping down her face. She looked down and saw it spreading down her shirt. She screamed, feeling again the pain of her dislocated shoulder. Frantic, she looked around for David, seeing again his crumpled form wedged in that impossibly small space left between the left-hand side of the car and the steering wheel.

A small part of her clung to the tenuous understanding this wasn't real, that she was just experiencing it all over again. Down the street, out of sight, she'd heard a minor fender bender, and the sound of metal hitting metal had sent her into a full-blown flashback. By the time Joel reached the corner and stopped the car, Carrie was coming out of the memory. Shaken and crying, she hastily pulled herself together, shrugging off Joel's obvious concern by saying she didn't want to talk about it. How could she ever want to talk about it? If she could feel it again, so real, so immediate, without conscious effort, what would happen to her if she actually tried to remember it?

Whenever a flashback hit, Carrie could feel a wave of terror approach her from behind and fling her headlong into the memory. Hopeless, she had no idea what she was going to do, how she was going to keep the memory at bay. It threatened her thoughts during the day and haunted her dreams at night. Exhausted, Carrie was so tired of feeling the pain. When was it going to stop?

It isn't just soldiers who experience the devastating déjà vu of PTSD. Any traumatic event in which a person comes to harm or believes harm will happen can produce PTSD. The harm can be to that person or to someone they know. PTSD can also be caused by witnessing a traumatic event involving a stranger. The shock of the event is so significant that it burns its memory deep.

A person suffering from PTSD is affected not only during a flashback, which is a vivid reliving of the event, but also his or her functioning is impacted day by day. People with PTSD may:

- startle easily
- become numb emotionally
- isolate from loved ones
- have difficulty with intimacy
- experience increased irritability
- become aggressive, hostile, or even violent
- attempt to avoid situations they fear will remind them of the trauma
- have difficulty during significant periods, such as the anniversary of the trauma
- refuse to talk about the trauma with others for fear of triggering a flashback

With PTSD, the person's life becomes hostage to the horror of the past. Like a person suffering from panic attacks, the PTSD sufferer stops living life and starts crafting an existence designed to reduce the possibility of another episode. Family, friends, feelings, risks, and experiences are all jettisoned. The avoidance of another flashback becomes the only goal.

You're Not Crazy

Within the throes of an anxiety disorder, you can feel like you've lost your mind. You can feel that you've lost mastery over your body, that it's become hijacked by a mind careening out of control. Your body and mind are on a wild, spinning ride with terror firmly at the wheel. You want to get off, but you can't seem to find a way out. You're trapped within yourself, screaming to get out, to make it all stop. You just want to find some place of normalcy again.

No, it's not just you, and, no, you're not crazy. What you feel and experience is real, immediate, and impactful. As you read earlier, such feelings are shared in part by forty million Americans. This isn't an unknown terror. While you will experience anxiety in shades and degrees, in circumstances and situations unique to you, you are not alone.

ANCHORING ACTIVITY

It may seem that our current, crazy, stressful lives produce a bumper crop of anxieties, concerns, and worries. Because we think our present circumstances are unique, we use them as an explanation and, frankly, as an excuse. We use them as an excuse to justify hopelessness, for staying stuck. *Life today is just so hard. This is something I have to try to tackle on my own. This is just who I am. I've tried everything and nothing seems to work. No one can really help. What I go through is just too weird; no one can really understand.*

Anxieties speak a language of absolutes. A possibility is a certainty. What could, will. What might, will. But if anxieties speak a language of absolutes, it is not a universal language. Some words are not translatable. Anxiety does not have a word for peace. It does not have a word for relief. It does not have a word for rest. It is a language of negativity, of hopelessness, of despair. It is a language of defeat. Anxieties force us to surrender before the true battle is even engaged.

There is an axiom: know your enemy. That's what I'd like you to do during this section. I'd like you to anthropomorphize your anxiety, your phobia, your panic attack and think about it as something other than yourself. This is a way for you to examine your anxieties and their consequences through an imaginary buffer. Put them outside of yourself and give yourself permission to examine them without triggering them.

Anxiety disorders have an anatomy. They have shared traits and unique features. What I'd like you to do now is get to know yours. As much as you're able, think of it in the third person. Use "it" instead of "I."

- Reading over the different descriptions of anxiety disorders, which one does it mirror the most?
- What are its physical characteristics? What does it do to you?
- How often does it happen?
- Do you know when it's about to happen?
- What do you do to help yourself feel better? Does anything help?
- Does anything make it worse?
- How long does it usually last?
- Have you ever talked with someone about it? If so, who and why? If not, why not?
- How long have you been hoping it would just go away?
- Do you really believe you'll ever be able to get over it?

Hebrews 11:1 says that "faith is the confidence that what we hope for will actually happen; it gives us assurance about things we cannot see" (NLT). Anxiety is a perversion of faith. Anxiety is the confidence that what we hope against will actually happen; it gives us assurance that what we can't yet see will be bad. Hebrews 11 is a chapter replete with the victories of faith. Anxiety doesn't produce any victories; it only accomplishes defeat. This is not the life God has planned for you. The life you're living now is not the one he wants you to live.

The faith life God intends for you is not the perverse life of anxiety. He does not want you to take your capacity for faith and distort it into a belief in the least possible or the worst imaginable. He does not want you to sacrifice your life on the altar of anxiety, giving up more and more year after year, hoping to appease anxiety's appetite. Instead of trusting in the catastrophe of today and the terror of tomorrow, God asks you to trust in him. As you continue to examine your anxiety and what effect it's had on your life, I ask you to transfer as much trust as you can from your anxiety to God. You've trusted in your anxiety's capacity to cause you grief, fear, and stress. Take a part of that trust and turn it over to God. Trust him to be with you through this journey, to know the face of your fear, to be strong enough to help you overcome it and loving enough to deeply desire to help you.

Meditate on Psalm 118:6, substituting the word *anxiety* for the word *man*: "The LORD is with me; I will not be afraid. What can anxiety do to me?"

Father, I am afraid! I live a life of fear, and I'm so tired. I have tried to deal with my fear on my own, but I'm not strong enough. I am overcome time after time. I confess I've never really trusted you enough to help me deal with my fear. I need your help, your guidance, and your strength. I confess I've placed more faith in the fear in my life than I have in you. Show me how to move that faith fully to you, each day, every day.

2

The Chicken Little Effect

Thought-Life, Hidden Assumptions, and Mistaken Beliefs

When I was growing up, like many kids I learned the story of Chicken Little. I don't really remember that it made that much of an impact on me as a kid; however, as an adult, I've found it amazingly insightful and have used it in at least one other book. If it were up to me, I'd subtitle that story *From an Acorn to the End of the World*.

In case you've never heard the story of Chicken Little or need a refresher, here are the basics. Like all good children's stories, the characters are animals. The main one, named Chicken Little, goes into the forest one day only to have an acorn fall on her head. Immediately she cries out, "The sky is falling!" and runs off to tell the king. Along the way she meets other barnyard animals with rhyming names like Henny Penny, Goosey Loosey, and Ducky Lucky. Together, they go off in a dither to inform the king of the impending disaster. On the way, they meet another character named Foxy Loxy, who offers his help to tell the king. What he actually helps himself to are Chicken Little and her friends, as he lures them into his den and eats them all up. Lovely children's story.

The sky, of course, wasn't falling; it was just an acorn. The danger to Chicken Little was not an impending celestial apocalypse. It wasn't even a small, hard object hitting her head. The danger to Chicken Little was her own panic-driven conclusion about the acorn. Perhaps, if she'd been less panicked about the sky falling, she would have remembered that foxes are not generally trustworthy where chickens are concerned (or hens, geese, or ducks, for that matter). By concentrating on the imaginary danger, she failed to recognize the concrete one. At the beginning of the story, before running into the fox, the danger to Chicken Little was an internal one, not an external one. This is the essence of anxiety-driven fear: the internal overshadows the external; the thoughts of what if overshadow the reality of what is.

Off to the Races—When Worry Has No Off Switch

It started small enough—a mole he hadn't really noticed before. It was on a hard-to-see place on Rick's upper back. If he hadn't twisted around in front of the mirror, he might not have seen it at all. Now, he took out a hand mirror and contorted his back to see it more clearly, while sweat broke out on his upper lip and panic raced through his veins. Why hadn't he noticed it before? What color was it? Had it always been that color? Was it changing? Changing moles meant cancer. He was at the right age for cancer to strike. Just last week, he'd learned one of his co-workers had been diagnosed.

Things had been going deceptively well in his own life for the past several months, so he was suspicious. Rick had been waiting for something to shift; maybe this was it. Staring at the mole intently, he tried to assess the danger. If it was cancer, what would he do? What would it mean? The obvious thing to do was see his doctor, but if it was cancer and he went to his doctor, he'd be living with the certainty and not merely the possibility. Did he really want to have his fears confirmed? Maybe if he just left it alone, it would be nothing. But then again, what if it was something? Did he really want to know?

If he did have cancer, wouldn't he have other symptoms? He had been tired lately. He thought it was just because of too many long days at work, but maybe it was something else. And his throat was a bit sore. Did that mean his lymph nodes were affected? He hadn't really slept well the night before. Was his body trying to tell him something? Rick's breathing was coming out in shallow gasps, and his heart was thumping uncomfortably in his chest. By the time he gingerly put on his shirt, so as not to disturb the suspect mole, he was feeling light-headed and nauseous. He didn't know how he was going to be able to concentrate at work, but what choice did he have? If he was going to become sick and die, he needed to work as long as he could to take care of his family. Outside the sun was shining and flowers were bursting with color, but as he drove to work, he saw none of it. The only thing Rick could think about was whether it hurt when he pressed that part of his back against the seat.

When Chicken Little got hit on the head with an acorn, she could have said to herself, "Ouch! I just got hit with an acorn! Next time I won't walk under that tree." Instead, she insisted, "The sky is falling!" Falling acorns are a natural occurrence; the sky falling is a natural disaster. One is common; the other is cataclysmic. When you struggle with anxiety, the common fast-forwards into the cataclysmic, and your mind controls the speed. Fear and anxiety are produced by what you tell yourself, not by what you actually experience. When your mind kicks into the fourth gear of fear, you careen out of the realm of the probable into the domain of the improbable. The field of the probable is narrow; the field of the improbable is vast. For this reason, it is very important to pay attention to what you tell yourself. This is what I call your thought-life. Some people have called it self-talk. It's what you say to yourself as you live out your day. It's what you say to yourself to interpret and make sense of what you experience. When fear takes over the interpretation, life ceases to make good sense.

Some people are very cognizant of this inner dialogue. They experience it as an almost-audible conversation. For some, this discourse takes on the voices of important people in their lives. For others, it is a near-constant internal debate, an ever-flowing undercurrent of thought. I call it *thought-life* because, for those with anxiety, it can take on a veritable life of its own. It colors everything you see; it drones in the background of everything you hear; it prods and pokes through everything you do; it rarely leaves you alone. You rarely feel you have control of it. For those with heightened anxiety, however it is experienced, the tenor and tone of this thought-life is almost exclusively negative.

I find it interesting that those prone to anxiety tend to ask themselves a lot of questions; they live in a what-if world. Like Rick, once their anxiety is triggered, they can go from zero (calm) to sixty (panicked) in under six seconds, and, generally, this process is accelerated through a barrage of questions. They question what will happen. What will it mean? How will they cope? What will? What could? What should? What might? On and on. The one thing they rarely do is question the questions. Are they valid? Where do they come from? What is the basis for each question?

From Chickens to Ferrets

It is my experience that behind each panicked question is a hidden assumption. Chicken Little asked herself if the sky was falling when hit by an acorn, to which she answered an emphatic yes! Here was a chicken taking a walk in the forest, presumably a familiar setting. Why would she automatically assume that a small bump on the head from above meant the sky was falling? Certainly this wasn't from personal experience. What was it about her thought-life that allowed such an extravagant assumption? Perhaps she needed to be a little less a chicken and a little more a ferret.

Ferret, as a noun, means a furry, little, burrowing creature. As a verb, *ferret* means to search out or discover. Behind the panic and heightened fear of anxiety is a storehouse of hidden assumptions—assumptions about the world, assumptions about yourself, assumptions about others. This storehouse is the personal repository your thought-life draws from as you interpret your life and your world day to day. The more positive and uplifting the contents of this cache, the more encouraging is your thought-life. The more negative and fearful, the more anxious is your thought-life. Uncovering this hidden trove of assumptions, then, is vital to understanding the basis for your anxiety.

As a teenager and young adult, Rick was significantly affected by two deaths. The first was the death of his father, who developed pancreatic cancer and died before Rick was out of high school. The second was the death of an acquaintance, a classmate who died in an automobile accident a year after graduation. The first was someone Rick loved; the second was someone he hardly knew. Both events made a deposit in the storehouse of Rick's thought-life.

When Rick's father got sick, it was a shock. He'd always been healthy, a vital man who did all the "dad" things with Rick growing up, from hiking in the mountains to shooting hoops in the front yard. He was a tough, manly sort of dad who wasn't supposed to end up sixty pounds lighter with sallow skin and sunken eyes. Watching the cancer claim his father's life over a two-and-a-half-year period made a profound impression.

Then, when he was away at college, Rick heard about Paul's death. He was still in touch with many of his high school friends, even though only two had ended up with him at the same school. Rick hadn't known Paul very well, but they'd circled the peripheries of each other's social sets enough for the news of his death to hit Rick hard. The solid ground on which Rick stood shifted once again, as it had in high school. While many of his peers viewed their future as an unassailable reality, Rick began to see it as something less substantial, more tentative, and less trustworthy. Fear had begun to soak into the contents of his thought-life with his father's death, and it continued to permeate following Paul's death.

By the time Rick was in his mid-thirties, fear had taken over his thought-life storehouse and turned it into a stronghold of suspicion. Fear tinged every thought; anxiety slid down a well-worn groove, gathering steam into full-blown panic. Molehills often became Mt. Everest, as Rick constantly worried about every aspect of his life. Worry left him on edge, exhausted yet wired.

People with anxiety spend so much time dealing with the present symptoms of their fear that they seldom are able to ferret out the root causes—the hidden assumptions—fueling those fears. Because those assumptions are hidden, they stay out of sight, whereas examination could reveal them for what they really are—assumptions, not facts or certainties or actualities. They are assumptions— something taken for granted. Things taken for granted usually bypass serious inspection. They are seen as rock solid.

The hidden assumptions behind your anxiety are no different. These are assumptions you have taken for granted. They've become part of your personal lexicon of absolutes. No amount of evidence to the contrary can displace them from preeminence in your thought-life. You are sure about them. You have not only the events of the past that have cemented them in your mind but also the weight of evidence in the present, as each negative thought rolls into the next, giving critical mass to these assumptions.

Although each person is different, with a unique mix of assumptions lurking behind his or her thought-life, I have found a common thread in many.

I am not worthy. One of the most insidious assumptions fueling a fear of the future is the one that says you are not worthy of good things happening to you. On the contrary, bad things happening to you is verification that you are not worthy to be loved, respected, blessed, happy, peaceful—you fill in the blank. When the foundation of your life and personality—how you feel about yourself—is shaky, your worldview and your thought-life are shaky. You distrust good things that happen because you don't feel worthy to experience them. So when good things happen, you wait for the cosmic equalizer to come in and balance the scales. In colloquial terms, you spend your time waiting for the other shoe to drop.

I am not able. This assumption says you are not able to handle whatever life happens to throw your way. Since you're sure it's going to be negative and horrific, you go through life terrified of what the next day (or the next hour or the next minute) might ask of you. Every day you wake up and worry that you'll find yourself crushed as a victim of circumstance.

I am not enough. This deep-seated fear comes from an assumption that you are insufficient in and of yourself. You live in fear of being left to your own devices, which you know to be woefully inadequate.

I am alone. If you know you are not worthy, able, or enough, you live in fear of being alone, of being abandoned by others. Even when in a relationship, you are fearful that it can't last and you ultimately will revert back to your exposed and naked sense of aloneness.

These negative assumptions undermine the foundation of your sense of self. Because they poison your idea of who you are, they poison your thought-life. Because they devastate how you see yourself as a person, you live in fear of suffering their consequences. To avoid suffering their consequences, you develop an intricate belief system aimed at mitigating their effects. These mistaken beliefs serve to cover over anxiety on the surface but only lead to an even greater number of fears.

Mistaken Beliefs

Within your thought-life's steady stream of negativity are personal proclamations of belief. They are things you are convinced are true, even when faced with evidence to the contrary. It is the conviction of the eighty-five-pound anorexic that she's fat. It is the assuredness of the addict that he has to have his drug of choice in order to live. It is the absolute belief of the fearful that disaster awaits.

Rick believed he would suffer a premature death like his father and Paul. It was no longer a matter of if but of when and how. As he got older, he became more suspicious of his future holding anything positive. Even the positive things in his life began to seem like a burden. If he hadn't married and fallen in love, it wouldn't hurt so much to leave his wife. That seemed to go double for his kids. Any promotion at work was viewed as something he'd eventually have to give up.

Even though he knew he'd have to give up these things eventually, he clung to them more tightly. It drove him crazy when his wife left to visit her parents without him, even though he was terrified of flying and wouldn't go himself. Whenever the kids left for school, he battled the thought that something might happen and they wouldn't come back. Many nights at work he stayed late, just to make sure nothing was left undone. He didn't want to leave any opening for disaster to enter.

Rick lived in fear of pain. He'd seen what physical pain did to his father over a two-and-a-half-year period. The images were embedded in his brain. He'd felt the pain of losing him and was sure he wouldn't be able to survive such pain again. His life became a constant lookout for the inevitable catastrophe so he could attempt to put it off as long as he could. In the meantime, on the inside, fear and panic were his constant companions. On the outside, he maintained a life, his family, relationships, work. He thought he was doing a pretty good job keeping a lid on things, but lately it was getting harder and harder to hide the fear. He felt as if the pursuer, who he always knew was behind him but whom he could never see, was gaining on him.

The hidden assumptions of *I am not worthy, I am not able, I am not enough, I am alone* undermine your personal foundation and sense of self. But people are very creative and adaptive, especially those living with the stress and pressure of anxiety and fear. To cope with these negative assumptions, people often construct belief systems that help them survive. Often these belief systems—and the actions that support them—are crafted in childhood. What starts as survival mechanisms, to mitigate the damage of these negative assumptions as a child, ends up becoming entrenched faulty belief systems as an adult.

Personalization. This belief system is based on the premise that it's all about me. Everything that happens is passed through a filter of how it affects you. You are constantly on guard for the negatives inherent in any event, no matter how seemingly distant from you. You see yourself as living in the eye of the storm. On the lookout for the coming disaster, you stay on red alert and watch for how circumstances and other people can or might affect your world. The belief is that everything can affect you and you are never safe. This is Murphy's Law taken to extreme—anything bad that can happen will happen, and it will happen to you.

Control. Personalization can lead not only to an awareness of how events, circumstances, and other people affect you but also to a need to control those events, circumstances, and other people. If events, circumstances, and other people have the potential to cause you injury, you come to believe you are safe only when controlling all of those things yourself, as much as you are able. The belief is that control brings safety. Lack of control, then, leaves the door wide open to disaster.

Perfectionism. If control brings safety, then control is paramount. Of course, events, circumstances, and other people are notoriously difficult to control. However, control can be exerted over something closer to home—you. You may believe that if you get as close to perfection as you can, then the possibility of bad things happening will be lessened. The problem with perfection is that it's an impossible standard. When perfect becomes the standard for safety, then anything less is disaster. Striving for perfection also requires enormous effort on your part—effort that is destined to fail. Not only is perfection impossible to achieve, but when it comes to your personal brand of perfection, it may not actually produce the effects you think it will. Perfectionism, perversely, does not mitigate anxiety; it multiplies it.

Dependency. Some people personalize the negativity of anxiety and draw it in to themselves in order to attempt to control it. They operate under the assumption that they're ground zero for disaster and that anything that can go wrong in their lives will go wrong. Taking this position, they take comfort in the certainty of disaster, if not always the particulars. Others will encapsulate the anxiety through controlling themselves and others. However, some people seem to go in a different direction. Instead of grabbing hold of events, circumstances, and people and drawing them into the sphere of self, these people do the opposite. They disperse themselves into the orbit and influence of others. They believe they are safe only when in relationship with others. Unable to establish value and worth in themselves, they borrow it. With their safety tied to others, so is their anxiety.

Affirmation. When you give other people control over how you feel about yourself, what they think matters. When you give other people control over how you feel about yourself, what *you think* they think about you *really* matters. Herein lies the catch-22 of a belief that others can affirm your worth as a person. Even when you give another person the authority to determine your worth, you still must interpret what that person thinks of you. Since you are already predisposed to think less of yourself, you'll be similarly predisposed to believe that person thinks less of you. The more positive things the person expresses, the less you'll believe them and the more expression you'll demand—and you'll be back at the beginning again. And those are just the positive things the person could say. This belief system, that approval of others is necessary for self-worth, leaves no room for the concept of constructive criticism. If approval is suspect, outright criticism is damning.

Out of Phase with Reality

Mistaken or faulty beliefs are out of phase with reality.

You are not the center of everything, the center of every bad thing that happens.

You cannot control everything around you, and, even if you could, bad things would still happen while you are in control.

As hard as you try, you'll never be perfect. And even if you achieve your standard of perfection, it will not conform to what actually is perfect because your standard isn't *the* standard.

Other people are not a reliable source for your sense of self-worth. They can certainly have input, but your self-worth belongs to you.

You are not able to gain universal, total approval from others. No one will agree with what you do and how you do it 100 percent of the time.

All of these mistaken beliefs are ways to manage anxiety; they are not methods to remove it. They are ways to manage anxiety, but they aren't very good ways. Instead of decreasing and de-escalating anxiety, they often serve to preserve it and prolong it.

Don't think it's possible to remove all anxiety and fear from your life. Fear is a physical reaction, and anxiety is a by-product of that fear. There are things in this world that you should fear, and over the course of your life there will be things that warrant your concern. But living with runaway fear and constant anxiety is not a healthy way to live. They blind you to the true dangers in the world, leaving you exhausted and unprepared when it really matters.

ANCHORING ACTIVITY

While it is not possible to remove all fear and anxiety from your life, it is possible to start evaluating the basis of your fears and anxieties and determining how grounded they are in reality. To evaluate them, it is important to uncover the hidden assumptions and mistaken beliefs you harbor in your thought-life. You need to pull them out and examine them in the light of reality. Hidden assumptions and mistaken beliefs relish the shadows; it is the shadows of your thoughts that give them power. Instead, you need to start really listening to them, get to know them, search out where they come from, and determine where they're headed if unchecked. You've been living with them in the back—and sometimes the forefront—of your mind long enough.

Before you start evaluating your own fears, I'd like you to practice with a couple of scenarios. For each one, think about how each of the mistaken belief systems might interpret events. As a refresher, the mistaken belief systems mentioned in this chapter are:

- *personalization*—accepting yourself as the epicenter of everything bad as a preemptive strike against the bad things you know are coming
- *control*—the need to control everything around you to reduce the number of and damage from the bad things
- *perfectionism*—the desire to be perfect in order to cut down on the number of bad things attributable to you
- *dependency*—using the shield of others to avoid dealing with bad things all by yourself
- *affirmation*—working for the favor of others so they'll continue to be your shield against the bad things

Scenario #1: You go to the doctor to have a medical test and are called two days later to say there was a glitch and the doctor wants you to come in to have another test. Under each of the following, what would you tell yourself?

- personalization
- control
- perfectionism
- dependency
- affirmation

Scenario #2: You read in the paper that federal regulators are looking into last quarter's statement put out by your organization's parent company. Under each of the following, what would you tell yourself?

- personalization
- control
- perfectionism
- dependency
- affirmation

Here's what I put for scenario #1:

- *personalization*—The doctor doesn't want to tell me the test came back positive (or negative, whichever is worse). The excuse about a glitch is just a way to get me back in to verify the bad news.
- *control*—I can't believe they are so incompetent! What's wrong with those people? It's such an inconvenience to have to go in again. If they're so incompetent, can I really believe the results of any test they perform?
- *perfectionism*—I should have been eating better and taking more vitamins. If only I'd exercised more, I wouldn't be in

this mess. Something's wrong and it's going to be my fault; I'll have no one to blame but myself.

- *dependency*—There's no way I can face this by myself. Someone else will have to go with me to explain what's happening and ask the right questions.

- *affirmation*—Does this mean I did something wrong? Are they mad at me at the doctor's office? How will they know if something's wrong if I can't do the test right? Will they still want me as a patient?

Here's what I put for scenario #2:

- *personalization*—I knew it. It was just a matter of time. The whole thing's going to come crashing down. I won't have a job, and, depending on how badly this thing goes, I might not even have a good reference.

- *control*—I can't believe they are so incompetent! If only they'd asked me, I'd have made sure there was no problem. Now I'm going to lose everything because of the ineptitude of people making five times as much as me!

- *perfectionism*—Did I do everything right on my end? Is there any way this can come back at me? I double-checked my figures, but what if I missed something?

- *dependency*—What's going to happen to my work group? Will I be separated from my co-workers? They know me, understand me; we work well together. If I have to get another job, I won't know anyone and they won't know me. I hate change. I know who my friends are now, but whom will I turn to tomorrow?

- *affirmation*—If I lose this job, people won't respect me. They'll think I'm a failure and won't want anything to do with me.

47

Now, stop and think about something: was it easy for you to identify with one or more of the five belief systems? When you read my responses, did any sound like a familiar voice? If so, identify which one(s). What part could you really identify with?

I wanted you to do this exercise because it's time to pay attention to the script of your thought-life. This is going to require you to be aware of what you're saying to yourself about yourself and the world around you. Most people, especially adults who have been listening to themselves for more years than they care to admit, don't stop long enough to really listen anymore. It's time for you to start paying attention.

To help get you going on this, think back to a recent event when you felt particularly fearful or anxious:

- What event, thought, or feeling have you chosen to remember?
- Do you remember when you first started feeling anxious or fearful?
- Can you remember what the trigger was?
- What's the first thing you remember telling yourself about this?
- What was your physical reaction?
- Did you try anything to calm yourself down? If so, did it work? If not, why not?
- What did you fear would happen as a result of this event, thought, or feeling?
- How immediate did you think this result would be? Would it take a few minutes, weeks, days, months, years?
- What actions (not thoughts) did you take in response to this fear?
- Looking back at it now, how likely is it still to happen the way you thought?
- Are you able to see any belief systems at the root of your fear?

• If you're able, take yourself mentally through each progressive stage of what if. What is the core thing or things you're afraid to lose?

I'd like you to start keeping an anxiety journal using these questions as a template for self-examination. Your task is to start to know the real you—the one deep down, the one that speaks to you in the quiet of the night and in the privacy of your thoughts. This is the part of you that has tremendous power over how you feel about yourself and the world. (If you do not feel able to work through this exercise on your own, please consider obtaining the help of a professional counselor to work through it with you.)

Philippians 4:8 speaks directly to the content of your thoughts. I really like how this verse reads in the *Message*. It says, "Summing it all up, friends, I'd say you'll do best by filling your minds and meditating on things true, noble, reputable, authentic, compelling, gracious—the best, not the worst; the beautiful, not the ugly; things to praise, not things to curse." It really does matter what you fill your mind with. I encourage you to engage each day in a positive moment. This used to be called counting your blessings. You'll need to do this each day as you begin to really listen to what your thought-life has been telling you. Fear and anxiety are not fueled by the true, the noble, the reputable, the authentic, or the gracious, though they certainly can be compelling.

Be intentional, after you've paid attention to the messages of your thought-life, to take a moment and fill your mind with the contents of Philippians 4:8. Ask God to help you call to mind the things in your life that are the positives, the blessings. They're there; you just need to see them.

Dear Father, reveal to me the messages that fill my thoughts and influence my heart. I need to know what they are, even if I don't like what I hear. Give me

*courage to listen and strength not to turn away or be-
come distracted. Give me a peaceful heart and a calm
spirit, knowing I am safe within you. Mold my thoughts
to become more like your thoughts. I need to hear your
voice above all others. Thank you for giving me courage
and a peaceful heart.*

3

Life in a Vise

The Effect of Stress

Marty found himself suddenly awake. Looking over at the clock on the nightstand, he saw it was 2:43 a.m. All around him was quiet. He could detect no reason for waking—no outside reason. Inside was a different matter. He was *too* awake, *too* alert. His mind was already zipping ahead to wake mode. Wake mode meant worry mode.

Lying very still, Marty tried to relax and go back to sleep, all the while knowing he would probably be unsuccessful. Once he was up, he was up—or at least his mind was. Already he was thinking about the ongoing demands and pressures of the day. Maybe that was what had awakened him initially—so much stress building, even while he slept. Now sleep was probably out of the question. Even if he was able to go back to sleep, the alarm would end up ringing all too soon and he'd awaken the second time groggy, irritable, and slightly nauseous. But what were his options? If he got up now, he'd be exhausted by early afternoon. He might as well just stay still and attempt to relax, attempt to shut off his mind, which kept veering off into areas that hyped him up instead of calming him down.

Alert and anxious, Marty listened to the thumping of his heart. He twisted around under the covers, trying to relieve the ache he'd just discovered in his back. Perfect, he thought to himself, another night of interrupted sleep. His tense body refused to relax, while his mind refused to shut off. Marty felt trapped and helpless, imprisoned, with himself as the jailor.

Anxiety produces a physical stress reaction. Adrenaline courses through the bloodstream, speeding up the heart. Breaths come out in deep, accelerated pants. The stomach twists and turns in gastro distress. The head aches, hands shake, pores sweat. Anxiety gets the body geared up for battle, poised for the classic fight-or-flight response.

This fight-or-flight response, in its proper form, is a good thing. It's what allows you to fly up the stairs when you hear your child choking. It's what prepares you to take an exam mentally alert and ready. It's what allows you to swerve at the last second to avoid the car that's just veered into your lane unexpectedly. It's your body and your brain running on all cylinders to address a stressful or dangerous situation. This response is meant to be protective and, often, it is. This response is also meant to be brief and sporadic. You weren't meant to live on red alert.

Under Siege with No Enemy in Sight

Long-term, chronic stress leaches health out of your body. What is protective in the short term is toxic in the long term. In chapter 1, you read a list of symptoms caused by various anxiety disorders. Those physical symptoms are centered around body organs or systems.

Your heart. A stress response to anxiety causes the heart to speed up. Often, blood pressure increases and your heart seems to be ready to burst out of your chest. This increased demand on the heart can also produce an irregular heartbeat called an arrhythmia.

Your lungs. During a panic attack, one of the primary symptoms is gasping for air, resulting in hyperventilation. This rapid intake of air provides more oxygen than your body actually needs and results in a corresponding drop in carbon dioxide in your blood. This drop forces your heart to work even harder. The faster you breathe, the more light-headed you feel. This can make your hands and feet tingle or feel numb.

Your stomach. Stress really puts your gastrointestinal system through its paces. The longer your stomach stays in a state of agitation, the greater the possibility of ulcers and irritable bowel syndrome. You can experience all the symptoms of a digestive system out of balance: indigestion, acid reflux, constipation, nausea, and diarrhea.

Your muscles. Many people manifest their stress in a specific region of the body, such as the back, face, or neck. The constant contraction of these muscles leads to tension and pain. The longer tension is put on these muscles, the harder it is to release the resulting knots and experience true relaxation, even in sleep. Some people clench their face and jaw muscles and grind their teeth.

Your skin. Anxiety has a way of returning your skin to a state of adolescence—skin prone to breakouts of rashes, acne, and psoriasis.

Your immune system. Stress is a little like the story of the boy who cried wolf. In this story, a young boy persistently sounds the alert, warning of a wolf. Of course, each time is a hoax; there is no wolf. Eventually, the townspeople ignore him altogether. So when a wolf finally appears, the boy yells for help but no one comes, with predictably disastrous results. When you are constantly under stress, you are yelling wolf to your immune system. Eventually, it wears down and can no longer respond appropriately to a real danger.

Your reproductive system. Chronic stress can result in painful periods and fertility issues. It's as if your body recognizes "now is not a good time" and reduces your chances for reproduction.

Your weight. Your body has a variety of stress hormones. One is cortisol, which increases blood sugar levels while suppressing the immune system. Its job during stress is to get you physically pumped up with energy and systemically less reactive. While this is a good thing if you need to race across an airport to catch your plane, it's not especially helpful in everyday life. Cortisol causes people to put on excess weight, leading to hypertension and cardiovascular problems.

Your head. Stress is painful, especially when it is manifested in chronic headaches and migraines.

Stress definitely comes under the category of "too much of a good thing." Each of these physical responses is designed to address a short-term, specific condition. What is meant to be effective for a period of minutes or, at most, hours becomes debilitative when that stress is prolonged over days, months, and even years.

Your body has an elaborate mechanism in place to address danger and stressful stimuli. Chronic stress, however, causes you to essentially stew in your own juices. Adrenaline, awash in the body and not used to address a bona fide physical threat, leaves you feeling shaky and weak. Cortisol, once released, increases your fat production and storage. The immune system, constantly under pressure, uses up its store of neurochemicals designed to balance moods. You are left feeling supercharged without any outlet to channel all that energy.

It is no wonder, with the range of physical symptoms associated with stress brought on by anxiety, that people often begin a search for answers and help with their primary care physician. It may not occur to them or their physician that the irritable bowel syndrome is a manifestation of years of worry. They may consider the outbreak of acne experienced in midlife a hormonal issue without recognizing the underlying cause of generalized anxiety. They may attribute the increase in aches and pains in the lower back solely to an increase in abdominal fat and not to a localization of stress.

The Chicken or the Egg

With all these physical symptoms, it can come down to the-chicken-or-the-egg question of which came first. Some people will be able to answer the question of which came first—their awareness of anxiety or the onset of physical symptoms. Hypersensitive to their anxiety cues, these people will remember vividly that first panic attack. They will be able to recount the year or the circumstance that initiated the onset of that deepening feeling of dread. Other people, however, may not be quite as sure. It will seem as if the physical symptoms and the anxiety have always been a part of who they are. The more anxious they are, the worse they feel. The worse they feel, the more anxious they are. It's a circular pattern that never lets up.

Whether or not you're able right now to pinpoint which came first, I urge you to spend some time in the next section really thinking about the physical symptoms you have. The ramifications of chronic stress are significant and need to be addressed. As you read this material on the physical effects of stress, you may have been surprised to see something you're experiencing but never attributed to anxiety. Anxiety is not just a "head" issue—it is a full-body issue.

ANCHORING ACTIVITY

I'd like you to take an inventory of how you're feeling—not just how you're feeling emotionally but how you're feeling physically. Take some time and really put some thought into your answers. Examine how you're feeling and be specific. Instead of merely asking if you get headaches, I'm going to ask you to answer with specifics such as when, how often, and under what circumstances.

Then using this physical inventory, work in conjunction with your primary care physician. (Please be aware, however, that pharmaceutical approaches are not always the best or most effective treatments available, and many have negative side effects. Only you and your doctor can decide what strategies are right for you.) If you don't have a primary care physician—or haven't seen one in years—I urge you to make an appointment. Bring this book and use it as a guide to discuss your physical symptoms. Get to know yourself and how you respond to stress.

Your Heart

Are you often preoccupied with your heart—how fast or how loud it's beating?

Do you find yourself worrying about your heart rate and stopping what you're doing to check it?

Is your heart rate one of the first signs you have of the onset of an anxiety episode?

What is your current resting heart rate?

What is your current resting blood pressure?

Have you ever thought you had a heart arrhythmia? If so, what did you do about it?

Do heart problems run in your family?

Are you worried about the health of your heart?

Your Lungs

Do you ever have problems breathing or feel you're not getting enough air? If so, how often does this happen?

Does this occur as a response to feeling anxious? If so, how often does this happen?

Are you able to regulate your breathing, or do you begin to hyperventilate?

During an anxiety episode, do you ever feel like you're suffocating? If so, how often does this happen?

Do you use a bag or other device to control your hyperventilation?

Do you have chronic allergies or bronchitis? If so, how are these affected during an anxiety episode?

How often do your hands and feet feel tingly during an anxiety episode?

How often do you feel light-headed during an anxiety episode?

Have you ever passed out or fainted during an episode?

Your Stomach

Do you experience high levels of gastrointestinal distress?

Do you often feel nauseous when anxious?

Do you ever feel a need to urinate or evacuate your bowels during or after an anxiety episode?

Do you regularly experience indigestion?

Do you regularly experience acid reflux?

Have you ever been treated for an ulcer?

Do you ever experience pain in your abdomen?

Do you have ongoing issues with diarrhea?

Do you have ongoing issues with constipation?

Have you ever been diagnosed with irritable bowel syndrome?

Do you experience recurring yeast infections?

Do you experience recurring urinary tract infections?

Your Muscles

Where on your body do you feel the most tension?

Does this tension go away with a hot shower or a massage, or is it constant?

Do you find yourself contracting parts of your body without realizing it? Do you clench your fists or tighten your shoulders or back?

Do you experience a high degree of pain in your muscles and joints?

Have you ever been diagnosed with fibromyalgia?

Do you grind your teeth at night?

Do you have TMJ or clench your jaw frequently?

Your Skin

Do you experience outbreaks of pimples, acne, psoriasis, or eczema? If so, which one(s)?

Have you noticed a correlation between your level of anxiety and outbreaks?

Have you ever broken out in hives during an especially stressful time?

Your Immune System

Do you feel a constant state of fatigue?

When have you noticed feeling better?

How long does that last?

Do you have difficulty healing from illnesses or infections?

Is there a particular recurring illness or infection that just never seems to go away completely?

Your Reproductive System

If you are a woman, do you experience difficult, painful periods?

If you are a woman, do you experience irregular periods?

Have you noticed a drop in your sex drive?

If you are a man, have you experienced an episode of impotence?

Your Weight

Has your weight been increasing?

Do you find yourself eating as a way to lessen your anxiety?

Have you been diagnosed with high blood pressure?

Have you been told you're at risk for cardiovascular problems because of your weight?

Do you find it difficult to maintain or lose weight?

Have you ever had a medical test to determine your level of cortisol?

Your Head

Do you get tension headaches? If so, how often does this happen?

Is taking an analgesic, such as aspirin, acetaminophen, or ibuprofen, effective?

Do you suffer from migraines?

How often do they occur?

How long do they last?

What works best to ease their effects?

Have you noticed a correlation between the onset of anxiety and the onset of either a tension headache or a migraine?

Your body and your mind, your physicality and your emotions are all intertwined. Each one affects and is affected by the other. The good news is that healing in one area promotes healing in another.

God made you a composite being—a person of flesh and feeling, of body and belief. You are a whole person—body, soul, spirit, mind, and heart. You are a body, and we know that when one part of the body suffers, all of the body suffers. According to 1 Corinthians 12:26, "If one part suffers, every part suffers with it; if one part is honored, every part rejoices with it."

What you feel affects how you feel, and how you feel affects what you feel. Your body and your mind are not at war with each other. They are linked together. You are a complex, integrated marvel created by God. Knowing and understanding how your body is affected by the stress you feel is an important step toward recovery and healing. Knowing and understanding how your body is affected by stress will allow you to recognize your own stress patterns and develop strategies to halt anxiety in its tracks and allow your body some real breathing room. It's never too late to make physical changes; there is always a benefit.

Holy Father, I thank you for this amazing body you have given to me. I claim the healing and capacity for health you designed in this body. Grant me understanding of my stress patterns. Give me wisdom to make positive changes so I can lessen the stress I feel in my life. As I think about my body, help me to focus on your power and presence shown in your marvelous creation, my body. Help me to make this less about me and how I feel about my body and more about you and what you've done for my body.

4

More Harm than Good

The Effect of Self-Medicating Behaviors

⟞⟋⟍⟋⟍⟍

Living your life on high alert is just plain exhausting. At some point, you want to find a little respite, a way out of the pressure and into some level of peace. It doesn't even have to be long-lasting. Besides, based on everything you've tried before, you've learned that's an unrealistic expectation. It does, however, need to be convenient and controllable. You want to be able to experience relief when, where, and how you want. It also needs to be reliable and predictable. When you're already anxious and wound up, the last thing you want is a disappointing surprise.

Most anxious people know their worry patterns pretty well. They immediately recognize the onset. They can feel things ratcheting up. In that moment of dread—fearing what's coming and what it will mean—a choice can be made. The choice can involve a self-medicating behavior to deal with the anxiety. These self-medicating behaviors—alcohol, drugs, nicotine, food, anger, or self-harming—can produce a relief, a distraction, from the anxiety. Over the long term, however, they come with negative side effects.

Self-Medicating through Alcohol

Patty felt keyed up, tense. Today, the plastic bus seat seemed harder than usual, and Patty shifted uncomfortably every few minutes. She felt like she was coming out of her skin and couldn't wait to get off the bus and get home. It wasn't that some*one* waited just beyond the front door but some*thing*. With the kids out and on their own—and her ex just plain out—there hadn't been much at home to look forward to. Over the past year, though, Patty had come to rely more and more on her evening buffer at the end of a long and frustrating day.

It had started out as just a glass of wine with dinner; after all, who was there to see or care? That single glass, however, had worked its way up to several refills. Patty stopped counting; she really didn't want to know. Cocooned in a merlot fog, Patty could feel the stress and worry that relentlessly stalked her during the day slip away. Nothing really mattered; nothing could get to her. The free-floating sense of impending disaster dissipated, merging with the fog. Fear, stress, and anxiety couldn't break through; she made sure of that as she topped off her glass. Of course, joy, peace, and satisfaction had no chance of scaling the alcohol wall either, but Patty didn't care, or at least she told herself she didn't. Everything in life came with a payoff and a payment. The payoff was numbness and relief. The payment was peace. For now, it was an acceptable trade.

"Relax; have a drink." We've all probably heard this more than once. We've heard it and seen the relaxation benefits of alcohol. Alcohol, it's true, is a depressant that works on the brain to produce a sense of relaxation. The line for relaxation with alcohol, though, is a fine one. The more alcohol consumed, the less benign the effects.

With the initial wave of relaxation can come disruption of sleep patterns, loss of physical coordination, loss of inhibition, slurred speech, nausea, thirst, fatigue, and dizziness. What starts out as a way to relax leads to a risk of developing alcohol dependence. What starts out as something you want turns into something you need.

Alcohol dependence is defined by the National Cancer Institute, part of the National Institutes of Health, as, "a disease in which a person craves alcohol, is unable to limit his or her drinking, needs to drink greater amounts to get the same effect, and has withdrawal symptoms after stopping alcohol use. Alcohol dependence affects physical and mental health, and causes problems with family, friends, and work. Also called alcoholism."[1]

Anxiety can produce a need for relief. When alcohol is chosen as that relief agent, it can be effective in the short term. But the short-term nature of that relief means you must continually use alcohol to maintain that effect. The more alcohol you use, the greater tolerance you develop for its effects. The greater the tolerance, the more alcohol you have to use to achieve the same effect. This is the vicious cycle of alcohol dependence.

What started out as a way for you to self-medicate your anxiety can quickly come back to haunt you. Your head choice for anxiety relief can become a physical necessity for anxiety relief. In the terrible paradoxes of addiction, withdrawal from alcohol dependence produces increased levels of anxiety. You started out drinking to help with the anxiety, and you end up drinking more and more because of the anxiety produced if you don't. You started out using alcohol to alleviate life's anxieties, and you end up adding alcohol-induced anxieties if you stop. Not much of a bargain really.

Self-Medicating through Illicit Drugs

Reilly shut his eyes and desperately tried to tune out his mother's rants. Why couldn't she just shut up and leave him alone? He had enough to deal with without all her complaining. It seems complaining was all she did anymore—complain and nag—all in a strident, high-pitched voice that reverberated in the hallway outside his locked door. She wanted to know when he was coming out, when he was going to get serious about going back to school, when he was going to get a job and start contributing to the family. He had no answers to any of those questions. That was the problem; that was the reason he stayed locked in his room as much as he could, smoking pot and trying to forget his lack of answers.

It seemed like the weight of the world was unceremoniously dropped on his shoulders as soon as the high school graduation ceremony ended. He was required to live up to everyone's expectations of what he should do and who he should be. But Reilly had no answers. He didn't really know what he wanted to do—let alone what he *should* do—or even who he was. High school had given him the identity of student. That identity was no longer attractive. He had put up with twelve years of school, and thinking about going to a college environment gave him the sweats.

High school was free; college cost money. His parents would expect a return on that investment. His parents would expect him to help pay. That meant a job. That meant working for other people. That meant doing what other people told him to do. That meant other people telling him he wasn't good enough. The thought of it sent his stomach into a tailspin. Wiping the sweat off his face, he took in a deep drag, willing the weed to block out this latest round of maternal venting, which appeared to be winding down. Reilly recognized the tone of futility replacing rage in his mother's voice.

Go away, he said to himself. *Why can't you just leave me alone?* With a sense of despair, he realized he wasn't saying that only to his mother; he was saying it to himself. He was just so tired of living like this, afraid to move in any direction for fear it would turn out badly. Pot was the only thing that kept the shakes at bay. He couldn't come up with any other way. Reilly's locked door was turning into less an act of defiance and more a signal of surrender.

According to the National Institute of Drug Abuse, marijuana is the most commonly used illicit drug in the United States.[2] It's relatively easy to obtain, relatively cheap to purchase, and has a certain social cachet. Its reputation as harmful is hotly debated, usually by those who use it consistently. The active chemical in marijuana is abbreviated THC. When smoked, THC travels from the lungs into the bloodstream and from there to all the body's major organs. When THC hits the brain, it produces a high, affecting the pleasure centers. The other brain functions influenced by THC are memory, thought processes, concentration, sensory perceptions, time sense, and bodily coordination. For something called relatively harmless, it has an extremely powerful effect. It is possible to become physically dependent on THC just like alcohol. And just like alcohol, when you begin to wean yourself off pot, the withdrawal symptoms can include heightened anxiety, along with irritability, decreased appetite, sleep pattern disturbances, and depression. A little pot has a way of metastasizing into more, sometimes much more.

Marijuana, of course, isn't the only illicit drug available; new varieties find their way to market on a regular basis. There is, however, a common thread throughout the currently available crop of illicit drugs, such as cocaine, amphetamines, methamphetamines, heroin, ecstasy, crack, and crank. The common thread is increased anxiety associated with using the drug. These drugs do not decrease anxiety; they increase it. Using drugs can produce physical symptoms that mimic a panic attack, such as rapid heart rate, insomnia, increased blood pressure, and feelings of paranoia. This is a drug-induced panic attack that sends your body into overdrive. A body in drug-induced overdrive does not have the ability to slow down on its own.

Self-Medicating through Prescription Drugs

Pam hurriedly finished up her work so she could take lunch early. She didn't want to be late to her appointment. Seeing the doctor was too important. Seeing the doctor meant getting a refill on her pain medication, which was absolutely essential. Before she left, she reminded her co-worker of the appointment and explained she'd be back as soon as she could.

Pam made sure to spread out her doctor's appointments, choosing early morning, evening, and weekend appointments so no one got suspicious of how many she had. Pam didn't have one doctor; she had three. One of the doctors thought she was reducing her pain medication. Before long, she'd need to stop seeing him, allowing him to think she didn't need the medication anymore. Then she'd have to find someone new to replace him, but she was getting pretty good at that. The doctors she used were kept carefully segregated from one another so Pam could continue to get what she needed, in the quantities she needed, without having to explain or argue. She was, of course, willing to lie.

She rarely had to lie to this doctor anymore. Her visits were perfunctory, just so the doctor could show he'd seen her before giving her a refill. A box checked off, a requirement filled along with the prescription, and Pam was on her way. She'd come up with this system when she'd started to use her medication at a much faster rate than prescribed. Pam found that the time-release tablets she'd been given were much more effective if she crushed them up, disturbing the outer coating and allowing the drug to enter her system rapidly. It took effect more quickly, but that effect then wore off more quickly, requiring more drugs. Good thing there were more doctors willing to prescribe them.

There was a time when Pam had been a little in awe of doctors, adhering to their instructions to the letter. But that was before the surgery and the pain that followed. Even after the pain was gone, the concern and worry remained. Pam was terrified of dealing with the aftermath of her health crisis unsupported by the medication she'd come to require. After all, it was her need, her body. Shouldn't she be able to determine what she took and why? She needed the medication and was going to continue to make sure she got it, whatever it took. It wasn't like she was doing anything wrong. These were her drugs, prescribed for her by licensed physicians. It was her name on the bottle.

Illicit drugs aren't the only ones with the potential for abuse. In our society, with advanced medical technology and pharmaceutical breakthroughs, people have access to a dizzying array of prescription medications. When used properly, in conjunction with a reputable physician, these drugs can be a true blessing. They should, however, be approached extremely carefully. It can be so easy to use daily instead of as needed. It can be so easy to look for another doctor to get another prescription. It can be so easy to neglect informing one doctor of what another has prescribed. This is the danger of using prescription drugs to self-medicate. When you become your own doctor, determining your own usage and your own combinations, you enter a highly dangerous arena.

Not every drug lends itself to self-medication. Certain categories have been shown to represent the greatest risk. These are pain relievers (such as Percocet, Demerol, Vicodin, or OxyContin), tranquilizers (such as benzodiazepines), stimulants (such as Ritalin), and sedatives (such as Seconal). If you want to know the latest drug that's joined the abuse category, just ask a police officer what is found at the local high school.

While we're still in the realm of prescription drugs, I'd also like you to consider the potential for self-medicating through over-the-counter medications. After all, these can be obtained in any grocery or drugstore. No need to answer to a physician. With self-checkout stations, there's no longer any need to answer to a store clerk. Just scan your cough syrup or cold medicine or antihistamine and be on your way, with no one the wiser to what you're really doing. Often, these products are used to self-medicate anxiety, especially at night. Taken in large enough doses, they have the ability to produce an altered sleep state, a drugged sleep state, all perfectly legal. When anxiety attacks in the evening and robs you of sleep, sending you into hours of panic and fear, going beyond the recommended dose or purpose seems a small price to pay.

False Support

When drugs, in whatever form, are used to mitigate feelings of anxiety, worry, and dread, the relief is short-lived and the long-term side effects are debilitating. These side effects certainly include physical effects. The body's built-in mechanisms for emotional and physical stability are chemically stripped and depleted. This damage hampers efforts at recovery. It keeps you chained to your self-medication regimen, even when you recognize it's doing more harm than good. The withdrawal symptoms of these drugs, including increased anxiety, chains them tighter and tighter to you. As I said earlier, drugs are no bargain; they come with a heavy burden that becomes more difficult to carry with each passing day.

If the physical burden is not enough to convince you of the true nature of these self-medicating drugs, consider their other side effects. All of us exist in a web of relationships, with ourselves, our thoughts and emotions, the people we love, the people we are in contact with through work, school, religious organizations, and social settings. Self-medicating through drug use takes a toll in all these areas and makes it harder to reach outside yourself to find answers, solutions, and help for anxiety.

Self-medicating through drugs doesn't just numb the pain; it numbs you. You lose touch with who you are, what you really think, and what you really feel. You lose touch with your emotional self. It's as if you've traded away all of who you are to get rid of part of who you are. It's as if you've forgotten that there's more to you than the anxiety and worry and fear. But when you jettison all of who you are in exchange for the numbing, transitory relief provided by drugs, you've counted who you are apart from the anxiety as worthless. You've thrown away your hopes and dreams, your aspirations and motivations, your drive and your determination in a bid to rid yourself of your anxiety. Bit by bit, use by use, you're carving yourself up and throwing yourself away. And the more you throw away, the harder it is to find yourself again.

Another casualty of self-medicating through drugs is your relationships. When you tie yourself to the drugs, you unhook yourself from other people. Other people, unpredictable, irritating, unreliable, become a distant second to the predictability of your drug of choice. Other people ask questions; they give their opinions; they stick their noses where they don't belong. Often, the people closest to you ask the hardest questions. They want to know why you've shut them out of your life. They want to know when you'll get help and stop. They want to know where all the money is going.

Other people get in the way of the primary relationship you've created with the drug. They keep forcing you to make a choice and then express disappointment, hurt, frustration, and anger when your choice isn't them. All of this concern and frustration just makes you cling tighter to your drug. Even thinking about the other people in your life—what they want, what they think, what they might do—makes you anxious. It becomes easy to assign them a role in what you're doing. It becomes easier to blame them rather than to consider your own responsibility. Blame long enough, isolate long enough, use long enough, and those meddling relationships can begin to suffocate and die.

Self-Medicating through Nicotine

Dave fought down the panic, telling himself to hold on, that it was only a few more minutes. The adrenaline surge of the panic kept shooting through his body, venting into anger. It was unfair, ridiculous really, that he couldn't have a cigarette. He remembered all too clearly what it used to be like to have an ashtray at his desk. Now every place was smoke free. He couldn't smoke on the job, he couldn't smoke at a restaurant, he couldn't even smoke in a public park, for heaven's sake!

It was so hypocritical—other people had their crutches. The guy in the next office lived with a coffee cup in his hand. The woman down the hall ate nonstop during the day—in her office, in plain view. He, on the other hand, had to wait until break time to go outside, in the cold and the rain, to have a measly cigarette. The discrimination was amazing; Dave couldn't understand how others didn't see it.

Just a few minutes more, he told himself as he hyperventilated, sweated, and watched the clock. It had been a stressful morning, and the only thing that was going to calm him down was a smoke, maybe two. Work was stressful enough as it was without the looming departmental audit. Productivity—it was all about productivity. They'd laid off two people and were trying to pressure everyone else into taking up the slack. The whole thing made him sick to his stomach.

Finally, it was time. Dave grabbed his coat, with his pack of cigarettes and lighter zipped up in the pocket, and rushed outside. He couldn't believe his hands were shaking; it had been a tough morning. Inhaling the smoke deep into his lungs, Dave willed himself to relax. For the next ten minutes, everything was going to be okay.

Smoking has long been used as a way to handle anxiety. When people get anxious, they smoke. It gives them something to do, something to do with their mouth and their hands. It provides a predictable, soothing action to help relieve the anxiety. Nicotine, delivered to the brain through smoking, can have a calming effect. Just the relief from nicotine deprivation can be soothing. Again, however, those benefits are short-lived with anxiety crouching close.

Nicotine, as a stimulant, can increase heart rate and blood pressure. The damaging effects of smoking on lung capacity can produce shortness of breath. Increased heart rate, a rise in blood pressure, and shortness of breath can mimic the symptoms of a panic attack. A link has been established between cigarette smoking and anxiety disorders in young adults and adolescents.[3] The very symptoms you use smoking to alleviate can be triggered by smoking.

So smoke to relieve anxiety and you could end up experiencing more. Smoke to relieve anxiety for a time and then decide to quit and increased anxiety is a virtual guarantee. Once again, the short-term relaxation comes with a high price. Withdrawal from nicotine increases anxiety. It's the same with all these self-medicating behaviors—a short-term fix produces a long-term complication.

Self-Medicating through Food

Robin could feel herself relax with the first bite. This is just what she needed. Taking her knife, she spread more butter on the soft, steaming bread and exhaled deeply. While she ate, Robin gave herself permission to think only about the food and how good it tasted. This was her comfort; this was her happy place where worries and cares and concerns were forcefully excluded. Her love of food was the only thing strong enough to keep out the dark thoughts. Oh, she knew there'd be time enough for them later, but for now she was at peace. The television was set to her preferred 7:00 p.m. show; the dog was sitting, tongue out, at the side of her chair. And on the table was her favorite fried chicken meal, the one that came with sweet corn, mashed potatoes and gravy, and a biscuit. It was the biscuit she always ate first because it was best when piping hot. She had chocolate cake for dessert, but that didn't make her rush through this meal. She needed some relaxation, some comfort. The chocolate cake could wait; it wasn't going anywhere and neither was she.

All day, Robin had felt unsettled, ill at ease, certain something bad was waiting for her right around the corner. Nothing had occurred that fit the bill, so she assumed whatever it was just hadn't hit yet. A thought went flitting through her mind that maybe her subconscious was trying to tell her something. Had she forgotten to do something important? Had she turned in something wrong and hadn't realized it? Was there something coming up that she needed to do but wasn't remembering? A stab of panic hit her stomach, interfering with the biscuit. No, she said to herself, not now. Taking her fork, she dug into the mound of mashed potatoes, making sure to scoop up a generous covering of gravy. There, that was much better. The savory gravy and the smooth mashed potatoes slid down her throat like a balm. She immediately felt better.

"Oh, no," she told her dog, whose eyes were on alert and whose expression was hopeful. "You'll have to wait. This is just for me."

Having worked with eating disorders for over twenty-five years, I have seen the connection between food and self-medication. Food is a powerful medicine. It is readily available and can be highly personalized, conformed to your exact specifications. It is tailor-made for self-medication, especially when self-medicating for feelings of anxiety and worry, because food produces intense feelings of comfort.

From our first moments of life outside the womb, food has been associated with comfort. Being hungry is uncomfortable, even painful. Being fed is relief. When you were a child, you probably had something given to you to eat as a way to provide comfort—or wish you did. Hurt yourself? Get a cookie. Do well? Have some candy. Food, for most of us, has always been around as a mood-altering mechanism, given to make us feel better or to serve as a reward.

Anxiety and the feelings it produces can be susceptible to food-as-remedy. One of the hallmarks of anxiety is gastrointestinal distress. Our stomachs hurt; they feel strange. We turn to food to settle them down, to make them feel better. We grab our favorite snack to make the flutters go away. Eat enough food and we can become relaxed and sleepy.

Certain foods not only produce physical comfort but also offer up a helping of emotional comfort. That piece of cake or warm, crusty bread takes you back to the kitchen of your childhood. That cake isn't just cake; it's the love you remember and long for. That bread isn't just bread; it's the relief of knowing someone else is taking care of you and will make everything better. Sometimes food was the only thing that provided you any sort of relief in a turbulent and chaotic childhood. Food and smells mingle in the mind along with emotions and feelings. They become intertwined and, sometimes, inseparable.

This enmeshment can lead to cycling. Anxiety can lead to food as medication. Food as medication can lead to overdosing on food. Overdosing on food can lead to obesity and health problems. Obesity and health problems can lead to increased anxiety. And round and round it goes. Just because food is legal and virtually on every corner, don't be fooled. It can be just as addictive for self-medicating as any drug.

Self-Medicating through Anger

Bill took the call, even though he really didn't want to. Why he'd given out his cell phone number to his supervisor was beyond him. Now there was no such thing as "time off." He was accessible anytime, anywhere. He'd thought about not picking up but instantly was worried about what the call might mean. He just couldn't take the chance. Better to know than not. With a resigned sigh, his wife shifted her legs so he could move beyond the noisy bleachers to take the call.

Putting his finger in one ear, Bill answered. Sure enough, it was as bad as he thought. He'd have to go back in to work; something about a hitch in the production line. Arguing would be pointless because he knew he'd go in anyway. With so many people out of work, Bill needed the job. He just couldn't risk saying no. Fear for his employment seemed to couple with his anger at having to leave the game and head back into town.

Walking back toward the stands so he could explain to his wife, Bill was furious. Why did it always have to be him? Why was he the one who had to fix things? Why did it always seem like he was low man on the list? Good thing he'd driven separately to the ball field. He'd made it through the fifth inning, so at least he'd seen most of the game.

When his wife saw him returning with that look on his face, she quickly excused herself and moved down the row to meet him. Already keyed up over the call, he was ready when she started in on what he always called her "guilt trip." It was easy to funnel his anger into pointing out all his reasons to go and all the reasons she should understand. Once again she was trying to make it his fault.

It wasn't his fault. He didn't cause it; he just had to fix it. There was always something wrong, and, as usual, it was up to him. No one understood what it was like worrying all the time about his job and taking care of his family. There were always a thousand things that could go wrong, and it would be up to him to find a way out.

As he walked through the parking lot, his mental battle raged. Whenever the worry surfaced, he felt sick; whenever the anger surfaced, he felt strong. Bill knew it was better to go with the anger. As he got to his car, so engrossed in his internal fuming, Bill missed the wave his son gave him from the dugout.

In regard to anxiety, anger can be both a consequence and a coping mechanism. When you are anxious, you feel more keyed up and less peaceful. When you're anxious, you can become out of sorts and angry. Anger is a consequence of anxiety. But if used intentionally, anger can become a coping mechanism for anxiety. When you are anxious, you often look to certain routines to help mitigate the worry and fear. Anything that disrupts your routine can be seen as a threat to your safety, a threat responded to with anger. Both anxiety and anger produce and use adrenaline. When that adrenaline is routed from anxiety to anger, the anxiety takes second position. Anger becomes predominant. Anxiety may have started off as the primary response to a given situation, but anger can quickly land in the driver's seat. Anxiety may have produced the adrenaline, but it can be hijacked and used by anger. Anxiety leaves you feeling out of control and vulnerable. Anger makes you feel powerful. Compared to each other, anger can appear the clear winner.

Anger, like all short-term fixes, may divert you from feeling fear initially but leaves you susceptible in the long term. The physical attributes of anger are much like those of anxiety. They are the fight-or-flight responses talked about earlier. Once the anger dissipates, the body is still in a heightened state, just waiting for the fear to reassert itself. Anger is not peaceful; it is not calming. It produces no sense of serenity. It provides no hedge of protection against anxiety. Anger and anxiety are physically related, and a person is able to move from one state to the other easily. Anger doesn't dissuade anxiety for long. Instead, it keeps the doorway open for anxiety to return at a moment's notice.

Self-Medicating through Self-Harming

Terry sat in the train station worrying. She worried she was at the wrong track. She worried the train would be late. She worried her daughter wouldn't be able to pick her up at the other end. Terry worried this entire trip was really a bother to her daughter, what with the new baby and all. As she worried, she mindlessly scratched at the scabs on her arm.

They were small wounds, kept constantly open by her incessant picking. Some of them were still fresh, fresh from her last round of worrying while packing to leave. Those she left alone. Instead, she looked for those that had formed a scab. The almost-healed sores were the best. There was something satisfying about working the scab off, feeling the twinge of pain and watching it bleed afresh. She always kept Kleenex handy to dab away the blood. It was why she wore long sleeves, to cover all the scabs and marks.

She picked at anything she could find on her arms, any imperfection, anything that felt wrong or out of place. It was pain she could identify with, pain she could deal with. It helped to override the anxiety and worry she felt so much of the time. The behavior had started with scratching and then, when the scratching led to a sore, had led to more and more sores, more and more scabs. Now she found herself picking at herself without consciously thinking about it.

She'd have to be careful, though, around her daughter, who hopefully would be too preoccupied with the new baby to really notice. This wasn't anything she could really explain, especially to her daughter. This set off a whole new thread of worry. What if her daughter found out? What would she say? How would she cover it up? If she said it was some sort of skin condition, her daughter might not let her hold the baby, which was the whole reason for going. Choosing an almost-healed scab safely on her upper arm and coverable by every shirt she had packed, Terry began to pick away. Nervously, she scratched the sore over and over. Focusing on the scab was a relief from worrying about everything else. This was manageable pain.

Self-medicating through self-harming is a way to use physical pain to cover over psychic pain. It's a way to feel cleansed of internal distress through the physical external release of wounding. Self-harming behaviors include making small, superficial cuts, burning, scratching, picking at scabs, hair pulling, and banging or hitting body parts. The physical pain is used as a relief and release from anxiety. It is using a lesser, more easily understandable physical pain to soothe a greater, more complex, indiscernible psychic pain.

Self-harm puts yourself on an altar of sacrifice in an attempt to appease intense feelings of stress and worry. It is your way of taking control of your own punishment by exchanging one pain for another.

Maybe you read about this particular behavior and shake your head in disbelief. Maybe you say to yourself you'd never do anything like that! But before you dismiss this behavior altogether, I'd like you to consider the ways in which you might engage in self-harming behavior. Maybe the scab you keep picking at isn't physical; maybe it's emotional or relational. Maybe you don't cut yourself physically, but do you cut yourself verbally, mentally? Those who engage in self-harming physical behavior leave physical scars. If your self-harm is emotional or relational, if it's mental or verbal, you're still leaving scars.

Self-Medicating through Holding On to Stuff

Ian could feel the tension rising as he made his way home from work. It had been a difficult day, and all he wanted to do was go home, close the door, and shut out the rest of the world. But before he did that, he had a stop to make at the neighborhood bookstore. This was a regular stop, an indulgence he permitted himself. After all, he worked hard. Some people spent their money on stupid things, like games or movies or clothes. Not Ian; his passion was books. Well, truth be told, it was more than just books. Ian devoted himself to pretty much anything in print. Since he was old enough to get a place of his own, he'd kept every newspaper, every magazine; he'd kept every piece of mail he'd ever received. Anything and everything in print was cherished, valued, necessary, especially books.

For Ian, information was power, information was pleasure, information was valuable. He never knew when he might need to know something contained in all those pages of print. It gave him a feeling of safety, being surrounded by all that information. Of course, it was becoming increasingly difficult to navigate through all the stacks and piles. He couldn't remember the last time he'd actually cooked in his kitchen because every inch of counter space was covered.

When his mother was alive, she'd tried to come in periodically and clean, but he'd finally put a stop to that. She had no idea how important everything was. To her, it was clutter, but Ian knew exactly where everything was—or close enough. She'd actually suggested he donate some of the books he'd already read to the local library, as if they stopped having value just because he wasn't reading them at the time. Ridiculous!

Even the thought of "cleaning out," as she put it, was impossible to entertain; it produced an immediate feeling of loss and panic. What if he lost something important? What if he needed it tomorrow or the next day or even next year? These books and magazines and newspapers were his hedge of protection that kept getting bigger every year.

I have known people whose houses were so packed with old newspapers, junk mail, worn clothing and shoes, discarded boxes, and used bottles and cans that it was virtually impossible to move around, unless using the elaborate walkways constructed through the debris. I've known people who had to start sleeping in their cars because their houses were unlivable—until their cars became so full of stuff there wasn't any place left to sleep. I've known people who reacted with abject terror at the thought of throwing away a grocery receipt or a dry cleaning stub. They kept all of these things to make them feel better.

People use all sorts of substances to make themselves feel better and ward off the world. They provide a sense of relief. They also have a way of taking over your life. Hoarding, the excessive accumulation of pets or things, is a physical representation of this emotional encroachment. Most alcoholics throw out the empties; smokers dispose of their butts; eaters take out the trash; drug users go to great lengths to destroy the evidence. Hoarders, however, are always surrounded by their self-medication. The value of this form of self-medication is not its use but its simple existence.

Hoarding has a chronology no different from any of the other self-medications. What starts out as a way to provide stability and relief eventually gains enough momentum that the person feels completely run over by it. When I work with hoarders to start letting go of whatever it is they so tenaciously hold on to, they experience an overwhelming sense of fear and dread. They are emotionally attached to the items, and discarding even one is like ripping off a part of their body; it is painful. They are terrified of losing the comfort they have so painstakingly imbued into each thing. When confronted with the need to start weeding things out, even with the promise that some things can be kept, they are mortified of making a mistake—of letting go of the wrong thing, something that will be needed later. Discarding has the ring of finality—a no-exit decision they'd rather put off indefinitely. It feels safer to keep control of these things, even if it means losing control of their lives.

Self in Control

All of these self-medicating behaviors are a way to exert control over the uncontrollable feelings of anxiety and panic. The greater the fear, the greater is the need for relief. There is a sense of help as well as a sense of helplessness. The sense of help comes with the brief respite provided by the chosen self-medicating behavior. The balm is there, however brief. The helplessness comes from a belief that the brief balm is the only one available. Relief, incomplete and tenuous as it is, is seen as inexorably tied to the behavior. Other options are suspect and do nothing but trigger anxiety.

I have seen people cling so tightly to these self-medicating behaviors, mistakenly believing this is all there is, that no other help is available. What they really cling to is their own obsessive need for control. Self-medicating behaviors are, at their base, all about self. As we've seen before, anxiety places you firmly at the epicenter of everything; you are ground zero. It's really all about you. Given this thought-life assumption, it's no wonder those with anxiety have a hard time trusting others and letting go of their own created and hand-crafted mitigations, their own self-medicating behaviors. The false sense of control created by these behaviors is an acceptable delusion, and because the control isn't real, the need for the delusion continues unabated.

ANCHORING ACTIVITY

Healing from the compulsion to engage in these self-medicating behaviors requires an honest appraisal of how well they are really working. You need to evaluate their true value to you and your life. Then you need to evaluate why you continue to do them, even when they aren't really working. In order to heal, you must honestly examine what your self-medicating goals really are.

In this section, I'd like you to think about and evaluate your self-medicating behaviors. This is not the time to be strictly literal. You're not looking for something that completely matches the scenarios presented in this chapter. Instead, think about each of the following and determine if and how you might be using them to deal with your anxiety. Write down how your anxiety and these behaviors intersect. Be honest and open about both what you're doing and what you're feeling. It is important to know how your anxiety is affecting these areas of your life, especially given how each of these areas ultimately has the ability to complicate and increase the very anxiety you're trying to lessen.

- alcohol
- illicit drugs
- prescription drugs

- over-the-counter drugs
- nicotine
- food
- anger
- self-harm
- hoarding
- other "secrets"—I've added this one because, as you evaluate your self-medicating behaviors, you may come up with one or more on your own. They still count, even if I haven't mentioned them. You know what they are and how you're using them and what they mean in your life. Include them. Be honest with yourself. Hiding them doesn't help.

Now that you've identified the behaviors you're using to deal with your anxiety, I'd like you to consider how well these methods are working. To do this, I'd like you to think about each of the methods you identified and how they affect the following areas of your life. Start first with the positives you feel these behaviors bring to you. However, be honest with yourself and consider both the short-term and long-term effects.

- How this behavior affects me physically in a positive way:
- How this behavior affects me emotionally in a positive way:
- How this behavior affects me relationally in a positive way:
- How this behavior affects me spiritually in a positive way:

Now think about the negatives these behaviors bring into your life.

- How this behavior affects me physically in a negative way:
- How this behavior affects me emotionally in a negative way:
- How this behavior affects me relationally in a negative way:
- How this behavior affects me spiritually in a negative way:

Finally, for each behavior you've identified, think about what it would mean if your life was no longer chained to this activity. For each, answer both of these questions:

How will I feel as I'm giving this up?
How will I feel once I'm free?

For many of you, these feelings will be different. The first answer may produce feelings of anxiety while the second may produce feelings of relief. The question you really need to ask yourself is this:

Are you willing to go through the first to experience the second?

These are important questions. Many people I've worked with have very much wanted the relief of the second. However, they were not willing to experience and move through the anxiety of the first to get there. They balked at giving up their preferred, terrible-but-predictable method of self-soothing in order to learn and practice other methods of anxiety relief. They were not willing to give up what they perceived as control. It was necessary for them to understand that this control was not their control over anxiety but their self-medicating behavior's control over them. Self-medicating wasn't giving them control; it was stealing it from them. Whether they acknowledged it or not, this loss of control contributed to their anxiety. Only by seeing the truth behind the behaviors were they finally able to unclasp their hands and let go.

Many people I've worked with thought they wanted to be free from their anxiety. However, as we began the walk toward freedom, they realized their anxiety wasn't something they really wanted to give up. It had become a part of their identity, a part of how they saw life, a part of how they interacted with the world and people around them; they had a difficult time giving it up. Instead, they wanted to learn how to manage and live (i.e., *control*) their anxiety, not live free from it altogether.

So as you think about each of these behaviors, think about what your life would be like without it. And think about how committed you are to doing whatever it takes to find freedom. Ask yourself, do I really want freedom, or am I looking for a more comfortable prison?

Don't be ashamed of your answer. You need to be honest with yourself. Understanding your real motivations is incredibly important. These self-medicating behaviors have a way of masking who you really are. It's time to come out from behind the mask and understand the truth behind these behaviors. Truth is always an appropriate place to start healing and recovery. Truth is really the only place to start.

Proverbs 12:17 says, "A truthful witness gives honest testimony, but a false witness tells lies." It is time for you to be a truthful witness for yourself and how you're handling your anxiety. So much of your self-medicating behaviors are ways to hide the truth, from yourself and from others. Start today to be honest with yourself and tell yourself the truth. There is strength in recognizing truth. There is freedom in recognizing truth. Jesus himself promises this when he says in John 8:32, "Then you will know the truth, and the truth will set you free." Truth will set you free, so don't try to hide from it; don't try to self-medicate it. The time for lies is past.

Loving Father, I want to know the truth about myself. I confess that the only way I can say this is because I trust you to uphold me in this truth. I need to know that you love me, accept me, and are here for me, even with the truth of who I am. Help me to love myself, in truth, as you do. Help me to forgive myself, in truth, as you do. Help me to see my hope, in truth, as you do.

5

Better You than Me

The Effect on Relationships

Collin walked up the steps to the porch, dreading what was coming. Jenny would want to know how things were going and what he'd done to fix what she continually called "the problem." The problem just kept getting bigger, and Jenny considered it mostly his fault. He'd been nervous about getting a house in the first place, but the agent had put them in touch with someone who was able to figure out a way to make it work. It worked, for a little while. For a little while he couldn't wait to get home. Now home had come to mean something else.

He vividly remembered the day they had gone in to sign the papers. He hadn't eaten all morning. Just the thought of owing so much money made him sick, but he was more afraid of Jenny's reaction if he tried to back out. In some ways, this house was his dream and his worst nightmare. He just hadn't counted on how quickly the dream would fade and the nightmare would kick in.

Sure enough, as soon as he closed the front door, there was Jenny. She didn't say hi or ask how his day was or give him a hug or a kiss. She just went straight to "the problem." Had he called like he was supposed to? What did the broker say? Would they be able to refinance? Could they get out from under the mortgage insurance?

When Collin mumbled that he hadn't actually been able to talk to anyone, that he'd left a message and his number, Jenny went ballistic. Her tone of voice scaled an octave as she berated him for not calling early enough, for simply not calling enough, for not demanding that someone call back. She recounted, for the umpteenth time, what would happen if they couldn't get out from under the mortgage, how they'd lose the house. What would they tell people? What would the family say? What were they going to do, live in an apartment again?

When the house had been a dream, she'd owned it; now she'd deeded the nightmare firmly to him. Jenny started to cry, but Collin didn't care. He was past trying to comfort her. It only seemed to make her madder. When she looked at him, it seemed as if she saw some sort of enemy. Jenny had drawn a circle of protection around herself, and Collin found himself increasingly on the outside.

In a wounded and furious voice, Jenny informed him she'd been so worried about "the problem" that she hadn't even thought about dinner. Collin softly said not to worry about it; he'd eaten late and wasn't hungry. The truth was he hadn't eaten at all, but he just couldn't stomach the thought of sitting down to dinner in the same room with her. He'd pick something up before he went to get Kenny from the ball game. It was a good thing Sarah was over at a friend's house again, so she didn't have to hear another tirade.

Collin had no idea how they were going to get out of this mess or what tomorrow might look like, but as he watched Jenny stalk out of the entryway toward the family room, he realized his thoughts of tomorrow and an end to "the problem" were beginning to contain less and less of her.

Anxiety exacts a stiff penalty on relationships. A person under siege from a constant barrage of anxiety has no breathing room to think outside of self. Every action becomes centered around relief from the stress and panic. Other people become either a necessary distraction or an irritating interference. Either way, other people stop being *people*, with their own feelings and opinions and actions and needs. When people stop being people, it means the death of the relationship.

A healthy relationship requires that each party bring something unique and special to it. A healthy relationship is when two people understand and appreciate each other. A healthy relationship is when value is placed not only on who you are together but also on who you are separately. When anxiety overshadows a relationship, it takes primary position by the nature of its urgency. Togetherness gets thrown out the window as anxiety diverts attention to self. Anxiety screams that self is in danger, that self must be attended to. With that kind of urgency, *us* is jettisoned for *me*.

Anxiety strangles relationships, but the ways this is accomplished can look very different. For some, personal anxiety can demand *relational isolation*. It's as if the person with the anxiety has a kind of relational migraine. Any relationship stimulus—even being around the other person—produces the kind of sensitivity avoidance that the worst migraine sufferers feel about light and movement and sound. The other person becomes an uncomfortable, and sometimes painful, irritant. As an irritant, the other person becomes a target both for the anxiety and for the anger, stress, and frustration produced by the anxiety.

For others, personal anxiety can demand *relational attachment*. It's as if the person with the anxiety develops a relational addiction. The relationship itself becomes a self-medicating behavior; fixating on the other person becomes a self-soothing technique. The relationship itself becomes paramount, not because of what the other person brings but because of what the other person blocks.

Both scenarios take a two-sided relationship and crush it into a self-centered, one-sided reality.

Relational Isolation

Living with anxiety takes a great deal of personal resources. Panic, especially, is an absolute attention grabber. It is akin to the all-encompassing pain of a migraine. For people who experience the stress of anxiety in this way, isolation is the only way to cope. Just as migraine sufferers must remove themselves from all outside stimuli, anxiety sufferers must remove themselves from all relational stimuli. This means that in times of stress—which they determine—they don't want any relational demands placed on them. On the contrary, they demand that the relationship place their needs first and foremost, but only when, where, and how they dictate. The relationship exists to serve self because, after all, it's an emergency; they're in pain, they're suffering, and "if you love me, you'll do this." It does not matter that the emergency is an internal one.

These people withdraw into self whenever stressed. These people demand that the other person be ready and available to support them without any thought of reciprocity. These people are irritable and moody. These people have multiple reasons and rationales for their behavior, each one emphasizing their need and minimizing their responsibility. These people expect everyone else to make accommodation for them; they live in the altered state of anxiety crisis. All of their being is focused on what they need to weather the storm, to make it through, to put an end to the panic and pain. On red alert, they promote themselves to captain of the relationship and demote the other person to deckhand, relegated to mopping up after them.

The stressed person is guarded and on alert while at the same time emotionally and physically exhausted. The other person feels under duress and, often, taken for granted and unappreciated. In such a state, intimacy is difficult if not impossible. Both people can feel put out, irritable, frustrated, and misunderstood. This leads to an even greater atmosphere of distance and estrangement. There is a sense that the relationship is broken because it is.

A relational migraine situation can certainly involve a marital or romantic relationship, but it can also happen between parent and child, siblings, close friends, or even co-workers. This is a relationship out of balance, with the anxious party overwhelming and consuming the joint resources of the relationship. It becomes a lopsided, one-way relationship that breeds resentment and disillusionment.

Relational Attachment

A person needing relational isolation says, "If you love me, leave me alone." A person needing relational attachment says, "If you love me, don't ever leave me alone." With relational isolation, closeness—emotional and/or physical—is rejected because of the stress of the anxiety. With relational attachment, closeness—emotional and/or physical—is demanded because of the stress of the anxiety. One person deals with stress by isolating into self; the other person deals with stress by merging into another.

With relational attachment, the overwhelming feeling for the other person is one of being suffocated by the anxious person. The anxious person needs to know where the other person is, what they're doing, who they're with. The anxious person bleeds that worry into the relationship, becoming suspicious about the other person, concerned about their fidelity, their commitment to the relationship. The anxious person needs ongoing reassurance that everything is okay. It is crucial for everything to be okay, for the relationship is everything. The relationship has become a coping mechanism for the anxiety and panic. The relationship allows the anxious person to be diverted from their worries, concerns, and panic.

This diversion requires fuel. At some point, it is not enough for the relationship simply to be "okay." Okay only goes so far. Stability is required; you want to know the ride is safe. However, a safe ride doesn't produce the thrill, the outlet, you're looking for. It doesn't provide a diversion from the anxiety.

It is akin to the relief felt by going on a roller coaster. Plunging down a vertical track at wind-whipping speed is just the thing to vent fright. The manufactured crisis of falling is a perfect diversion. You want the ride to be safe, but you also want it to be thrilling. A safe, stable ride just doesn't produce the same "kick." Relational attachment is much the same way. The relief, the self-soothing, is a balance between stability and crisis. The relationship must be both stable and in crisis, paradoxically. Stability is required to relieve anxiety through knowing the ride, the relationship, is safe. Crisis is required to relieve anxiety through diversion. In relationship attachment, the other person becomes your stable and diverting ride, one that takes you out of yourself and provides the momentary jolt of an out-of-body experience. When the body you live in is full of stress and anxiety and panic, you'll do just about anything to escape, even for a little while.

In relational attachment, the stressed person is on guard and alert, watching for any signs of shift in the relationship, which has become so necessary to provide an outlet for anxiety. The other person feels imprisoned in the bonds of the relationship, chafing at the constant scrutiny and irritated by the repeated demands to prove himself or herself. In this situation, intimacy becomes complicated. The anxious person may have difficulty expressing intimacy out of fear of rejection. The other person may resent the cloying nature of the relationship and withdraw from the intensity inherent in intimacy. Again, this relationship can be a marital or romantic one, but it can also involve a parent and a child, siblings, friends, or co-workers.

When Worlds Collide

It's said that opposites attract. The two types of anxious people outlined here are truly opposites in many ways. So what happens when these two opposites attract? It is often called codependency. The avoidant, isolated person will often be drawn to the attachment person and vice versa. The attachment person will be drawn to an avoidant person, recognizing the high potential for crisis, for diversion. The avoidant person will be drawn to an attachment person, recognizing the willingness to subjugate self for the sake of the relationship.

Codependency in anxiety relationships is further complicated by the presence of other self-medicating behaviors. I say *other* self-medicating behaviors because the attachment person is already using the relationship as a form of self-medicating, of numbing, of diversion. The avoidant person, as a way of isolating, may turn to self-medicating behaviors too. The avoidant person doesn't need the attachment person to self-soothe. Instead, the avoidant person needs the attachment person to facilitate and support the self-soothing, self-medicating behavior.

The more isolated the avoidant person becomes, the bigger the crisis, the bigger the diversion, for the attachment person. The clingier the attachment person becomes, the greater the need in the avoidant person for his or her isolating behaviors. Each one pulls at the opposite ends of the other. Each one ends up strengthening the other to the extreme detriment of both.

The Suffocation of Safety

Not every relationship is a codependent one. Anxious people are in relationship often with non-anxious people. These are loving, caring, compassionate people who end up occupying a difficult position in relation to the anxious person. They come to represent safety to the anxious person. This is especially true in a relationship with a person suffering from social anxiety or a specific phobia such as agoraphobia.

In social anxiety, it is the danger of crowds, of being with other people in strange and uncontrollable situations, that elicits terror and fear. This fear, however, is not all-encompassing. There are generally family members or loved ones who are considered safe, along with very specific situations. The safe person then becomes the repository of the anxious person's social needs and, quite often, physical needs because of the anxious person's refusal to interact with the world.

This person may be required to handle any and all social interaction the anxious person feels incapable of handling. This can mean being a buffer with visitors in the home or making phone calls on the person's behalf. Because of the acute nature of the social anxiety and the feelings produced, the other person may be given little choice about cooperating and being available. The other person takes on the role of caregiver for what can be years. And during those years, in the pursuit of caring for the anxious person, the caregiver invariably neglects himself or herself.

In addition to social anxiety, certain specific phobias can place a tremendous burden on relationships. The more common the source of the phobia, the greater is the burden. For example, if you are in a relationship with someone who has a specific phobia of snakes, this probably isn't going to have a significant impact on your relationship. You probably will decide not to vacation in the desert or take a canoe trip down a South American river, but there are plenty of places you can go with very little expectation of snakes. If you go to the zoo together, you'll simply avoid the reptile cage.

But what do you do about agoraphobia, the fear of open spaces? With an agoraphobic, your relationship may be confined, literally, to a single home or a single room within that home. In order for that person to feel safe, you may become as needed, as essential, as the safety of those four walls. As such, leaving that person has a physical impact. Your leaving may produce a panic attack on the part of the agoraphobic. This kind of relationship can be as suffocating and damaging as an attachment relationship.

What if you are the anxious person who has assigned such necessity to another person? As I said before, people are notoriously unpredictable and often unreliable. When another person represents such value to you and your life, it is impossible not to become possessive. That person ceases to have value for who they are when you place an even greater value on what they can do for you. The person stops being a distinct individual with his or her own needs and instead becomes a repository for your needs. People weren't made to be possessed by others; our very nature rebels against it. This represents a no-win scenario.

Anxiety, in whatever form it takes, damages relationships. It interferes with the normal, healthy growth and maturation of relationships. Anxiety places unreasonable and unattainable demands on other people, fueling resentment and a desire to escape. Anxiety fuels anger and anger fuels anxiety, causing collateral damage on relationships and blurring the lines between friend and foe. Anxiety narrows focus down to the point of self, blocking out the vision necessary to see and appreciate others. Anxiety may feel like it's centered around you, but it reverberates throughout your relationships, sending shock waves and weakening your relational bonds.

ANCHORING ACTIVITY

For this chapter, I'd like you to evaluate your relationships with other people. Start with those closest to you—family, if you have them. Then move out and incorporate good friends, colleagues, co-workers, anyone who is in a significant relationship with you. If you're unsure whether a relationship is significant, think of yourself tomorrow without that person in your life. If the absence of that person causes you pain—not merely regret but pain—the relationship is significant.

Make a list of your significant relationships. You can put down as many as you like, but try to put down at least five. As you evaluate these relationships, you'll be looking for patterns. The more relationships you put down, the greater the potential for seeing and understanding the patterns.

For the moment, I'd like these to be human relationships. A little later we'll deal with your spiritual relationships. For now, focus on the people in your life.

Once you've compiled your relationship list, I'd like you to think about the ways your anxiety affects each. Do you tend to exhibit avoidant tendencies or attachment tendencies? If you have difficulty deciding or thinking about the person in this context, try to remember a specific situation with this person that was very stressful. Remember back to how you reacted, what you said to this person, what you did. Answer these few questions:

- In what specific ways does your anxiety impact this relationship?
- Is your relationship strengthened or weakened by your anxiety?
- If your anxiety could be removed from this relationship, what would it mean to you?
- If your anxiety could be removed from this relationship, what would it mean to the other person?

Proverbs 12:25 in the *Message* says, "Worry weighs us down; a cheerful word picks us up." This is true individually, and it's true of our relationships. Worry, as the main component of a relationship, is a burden, a weight on that relationship. Of course, healthy relationships are not merely sunny-day relationships; they need to be able to handle a little rain from time to time. But all relationships need encouraging and cheerful words and actions. If your main contribution to your relationships is a constant addition of worry, they will eventually break under the strain if they aren't cracking already. You owe it to yourself to be free from your worry. You owe it to those you love and are in relationship with to share that freedom with them.

> *Dear God, you are the Father of relationships. You caused them to be and orchestrated their components. In your wisdom you created parent and child, husband and wife, sister and brother, friend and friend. Give me the courage to see and accept the consequences of anxiety on my relationships. Allow this knowledge to empower and motivate me to work through this anxiety, to heal myself and my relationships.*

6

Never Mind

The Effect of Depression

———⟨⟩———

Patricia lay in bed, dreading waking up, let alone getting up. At least in sleep she could escape for just a little while. Waking up meant gearing up, gearing up to somehow face another day. Patricia didn't know exactly how she was going to pull that off. Already she could feel her heart racing in her chest, as if ramping up for the effort. Desperately, she wanted to go back to sleep, back to oblivion.

But like always, once she was awake, oblivion shattered. On came the mental onslaught as all her worries and fears crashed against her in waves. On the outside, Patricia lay motionless in bed. On the inside, she felt she was thrashing against her fears, drowning in them. It never seemed to get any better. Why couldn't these thoughts just leave her alone? Why did they always have to come rushing back in? Why couldn't they stay wherever they went in sleep and never come back?

Glancing at the clock, she realized she'd been asleep for almost ten hours, but she didn't feel rested. Instead, she felt exhausted and keyed up, all at the same time. It was Saturday, and she could hear her neighbors out mowing their lawns. A dog barked, and she caught the squeals of delight from children at play. Although she couldn't tell by the darkness in her room because of the shades, it must be sunny out. Most people couldn't wait for a sunny Saturday; Patricia just wanted to stay in bed, stay oblivious and escape for a little while longer.

By now her heart rate was really fast, along with her breathing. If she just lay there thinking about the possibility, she'd be in for a full-blown panic attack. Better to get up and at least move through it instead of become lost in it. With a deep sigh, she got up. Looking ahead to all the activities of the day, she had no idea which one to tackle first or if it would even make a difference. Her goal was not to enjoy anything but merely to survive it, to get through it. Nothing gave her pleasure anymore; she was long past that. Instead, her goal was to minimize the pain, the sense of hopelessness each day seemed to bring. Since nothing ever got any better, Patricia worked at keeping everything the same—not better but not worse, just the same dull, gray existence. The gray was preferable to the chaotic, jarring swirls of riotous color produced by her anxiety. Her goal was to get through the day without having to think or feel. Thinking and feeling always led to anxiety, and she couldn't handle that, not emotionally, not physically, not in any way. Patricia was up and firmly in survival mode. She just had to get through the next fourteen hours or so.

Depression has been compared to a smothering blanket of no emotion, a shroud of numbness that settles over your soul. This is not a condition most people would welcome—that is, of course, unless you consider what condition is being shrouded. For some anxious people, depression produces a perverse sense of relief. Because of this, anxiety and depression can go hand in hand.

When depression is coupled with anxiety, it can be difficult to separate the two, especially when the emotional lethargy of depression is seen as an acceptable alternative to a stressful state of anxiety. Anxious people are very aware of their anxiety but may be less cognizant of their depression. Here are the signs and symptoms of depression as outlined by the National Institutes of Mental Health:

- persistent sad, anxious, or "empty" mood
- feelings of hopelessness, pessimism
- feelings of guilt, worthlessness, helplessness
- loss of interest or pleasure in hobbies and activities
- decreased energy, fatigue, being "slowed down"
- difficulty concentrating, remembering, making decisions
- difficulty sleeping, early-morning awakening, or oversleeping
- appetite and/or weight changes
- thoughts of death or suicide; suicide attempts
- restlessness, irritability
- persistent physical symptoms[1]

You'll notice that the first sign listed for depression includes the word *anxious*. As more is being learned about the link between depression and anxiety, a differentiation is occurring between depression without anxiety and what is being called *anxious depression*. When anxiety and depression are linked together, treatment becomes complicated:

> People with major depression accompanied by high levels of anxiety are significantly less likely to benefit from anti-depressant medication than those without anxiety, according to a study based on data from the NIMH-funded Sequenced Treatment Alternatives to Relieve Depression (STAR*D) study. . . . The results are consistent with previous research showing that people with depression and high levels of anxiety are less likely to respond to anti-depressant

medication, regardless of what medication is used. This also may lead to more recognition and possible diagnosis of anxious depression.[2]

The lead researcher in the study goes on to say that "the combination likely warrants a more personalized treatment approach."[3]

Stop, I Want to Get Off

I have seen firsthand the link between anxiety and depression. The possibility for the chronically anxious person to become depressed is real, and the reasons can be compelling. Earlier I likened the anxious state to being constantly on red alert. The mind and the body are in a heightened condition all the time. However, unlike the temporary thrill of a roller coaster, this ride never ends. Any relatively stable stretch only provides time to ramp up for the next neck-bending climb and heart-pounding fall. The cycle keeps repeating itself over and over. For some people, there comes a point when it all becomes too much; they just want to shut down. But if you can't get off and the ride never ends, the only alternative is to stop reacting to the ride. If the ride never shuts down, then they will. Unfortunately, the ride is their life. By checking out of the anxiety, they are checking out of life. Depression becomes a way to numb themselves, to check out, to experience relief from the chaos.

When the body and the mind are overstressed and taxed to the maximum by circumstances, such as ongoing anxiety, depression is a very real possibility. This is not a conditional crisis brought on by a single event or situation but a chronic crisis state brought on by the ongoing demands of anxiety. In some people, when their coping and caring mechanisms are depleted, they shut down into depression. Depression begins as a coping mechanism for anxiety but becomes intertwined with and strengthened by the anxiety. Both are fueled by feelings of helplessness to overcome and hopelessness of things ever getting better.

One woman I worked with put it this way: "When I first started feeling depressed, frankly, I was relieved. I just reached a point where, if all I could feel was panic, I would rather not feel anything at all." At first, she welcomed the shroud of depression as an acceptable antidote to the hyperstate of her panic. The weight of her depression, however, was not enough to tamp down her feelings of panic and anxiety indefinitely. Those stabs of sheer terror and worry began to find cracks in her numbed façade, only now she felt less able to handle them, struggling as she was with her depression as well. Even in the panic, she'd been able to experience brief moments of enjoyment and pleasure. With the depression, those were gone. It didn't take long for the anxiety and panic attacks to become even more pronounced, as her resiliency faded with the depression. Despair was now a constant companion, compounded by the failure of various medications. "If my family hadn't intervened and demanded I get help, I could have so easily decided to end things altogether."

I have also seen the reverse, where depression occurs first, followed by anxiety in the form of panic attacks. It's as if depression has leached out all hope, joy, and optimism from a person's life. Denuded of these life-affirming characteristics, the person becomes vulnerable to an anxiety attack. When the assault takes place, the person has no emotional stability to assist in placing the experience in proper perspective. A single, transitory fear, worry, or concern blossoms into a full-blown panic attack. Once that possibility, that potential, is activated, a new paradigm is created. Panic-once means panic-possible, forever. This kind of helpless feeling is in perfect harmony with the bleak outlook of depression.

Whether anxiety or depression occurs first, when combined, both will tell you things can never get any better, that you are helpless to effect positive change. They can appear like twin juggernauts, barreling down and flattening your life and your ability to experience relief. When these two are joined together, they create an even higher threshold for recovery.

Hiding in Plain Sight

Again, it is not immediately apparent that a person suffering from anxiety is also experiencing depression. Both can be chronic situations and, when combined, the symptoms difficult to separate. For the person suffering from generalized anxiety disorder (GAD), there is already a sense of being restless and irritable, easily fatigued, with trouble concentrating and sleeping. Because of a constant state of worry, activities can become less enjoyable, or even problematic, if they trigger feelings of discomfort, unease, or fear. Those suffering from anxiety have trouble making decisions because of the need to evaluate the decision against feelings of concern regarding possible outcomes. Anxiety, worry, and fear become a virtual backdrop to life, altering the norm and masking the signs and symptoms of depression. Those suffering from social anxiety disorder often are also depressed because of the isolation and self-imposed limitations on life and its possibilities.

The more event-driven aspects of an anxiety disorder can be easier to winnow out from depression. For example, the symptoms of a panic attack are very specific and unique. Similarly, specific phobias, such as those involving airplanes or water or heights, are situational, allowing a level of normalcy outside that specific situation.

To untangle a connection between anxiety and depression, it is important to seek caring, professional help. Again, as stated earlier, often people will begin with their physician, complaining of physical ailments such as rapid heart rate, fatigue, stomachaches, headaches, and a general feeling of blah. However, research points to a need for more than medications to deal with these issues. Start with your physician, but don't end there. Ask for a referral to a competent therapist or counselor as well. As the researcher quoted above said, the combination of anxiety and depression "likely warrants a more personalized treatment approach."

The treatment approach we utilize at the Center is a whole-person approach that incorporates the emotional, relational, physical, and spiritual aspects of a person, weaving all these together to promote long-term healing and recovery. This is the most personalized approach you can have because it is centered around you. Our treatment teams consist of mental health counselors, chemical dependency professionals, physicians, and dietitians. Because we are Christian-based, we include a spiritual component. Over the years, we've refined and used this model because it is the one that has produced the most long-term recovery in people's lives.

ANCHORING ACTIVITY

Several years ago, I wrote *Moving beyond Depression* out of a deep desire to help those struggling with overwhelming despair and hopelessness. It has struck a chord with many people I've worked with myself, as well as with those across the United States and internationally who have used the book in conjunction with local therapists and physicians. At the beginning of that book is a questionnaire I developed to help people identify whether they are experiencing signs and symptoms of depression. I've included it here so you can better understand if depression has become tied to your anxiety.

There are certainly all sorts of tools you can use to determine whether you're depressed. You can get them online, from your doctor, from books, even from family or friends. The following indicators are gleaned from our experiences at the Center, and the diagnostic definitions are from a whole-person point of view. As you look over these indicators, note any that describe your own feelings.

Yellow indicators can include conditions that have been present in your life for a long time, even a number of years. Red indicators come from the established criteria for clinical depression and, because of the severity, can have a much shorter duration.

Yellow Indicators

- a loss of enjoyment in established activities
- feeling restless, tired, or unmotivated at work
- an increase in irritability or impatience
- feeling either wound up or weighed down
- feeling overburdened with life and its activities
- a lack of spiritual peace or well-being
- finding relief by controlling aspects of your personal behavior, including consuming liquids or food
- a fear of expressing strong emotions
- a constant anxiety or vague fear about the future
- feeling unappreciated by others
- feeling a sense of martyrdom as if you are constantly asked to do the work of others
- exercising a pattern of impulsive thinking or rash judgments
- a loss of interest in sexual activities or sexual difficulties
- a sense of enjoyment at seeing the discomfort of others
- anger at God for how you feel
- a recurrent pattern of headaches, muscle aches, body pains
- feeling social isolation and distancing from family or friends
- feeling trapped during your day by what you have to do
- displaying a pattern of pessimistic or critical comments and/ or behaviors
- feeling like your best days are behind you and the future doesn't hold much promise

- feeling left out of life
- bingeing on high-calorie foods to feel better
- apathetic upon waking about how the day will turn out
- feeling it is easier to do things yourself instead of wanting to work with others
- experiencing recurring gastrointestinal difficulties
- feeling trapped inside your body
- dreading the thought of family get-togethers or social gatherings
- feeling overweight, unattractive, or unlovable
- feeling old, discarded, without value
- feeling unmotivated to try new activities, contemplate new ideas, or enter into new relationships

Red Indicators

- a significant change in appetite, lasting longer than two weeks, resulting in either marked weight loss (if not dieting) or weight gain
- recurring disturbances in your sleep patterns for longer than two weeks resulting in difficulty falling and staying asleep or sleeping too much
- increased agitation or inability to relax occurring for an extended period of time (over two weeks)
- feelings of fatigue, lethargy, or loss of energy occurring for an extended period of time (over two weeks)
- feelings of sadness, despondency, despair, loneliness, or worthlessness ongoing for an extended period of time (over two weeks)
- an inability to concentrate, focus, or make decisions recurring over a period of time (over two weeks)

- recurring thoughts of death or suicide
- planning or attempting a suicide

If, after completing this inventory, you recognize several yellow and, certainly, any red indicators, I urge you to seek professional help immediately. While anxiety and depression complicate each other, both can be successfully identified and addressed. They don't need to compose the overriding themes for your life, drowning out life itself.

The New Living Translation of the Bible puts Ecclesiastes 2:22–23 this way: "So what do people get in this life for all their hard work and anxiety? Their days of labor are filled with pain and grief; even at night their minds cannot rest. It is all meaningless." Our loving Father did not create you to live a meaningless life full of anxiety, pain, and grief. This is the life hijacked by anxiety and depression. In John 10:10, Jesus says he came so that we may have "a rich and satisfying life" (NLT). This is what he wants for you, but if you are not able to create this for yourself, you must look to others to help you. Asking for help is not an admission of defeat; asking for help is a statement of victory over helplessness and hopelessness. Asking for help isn't giving up who you are; asking for help helps you find who you are.

Father God, I need your help. Allow me to trust in you and believe that help is available for me. Help me not to give in to hopelessness and despair. Give me the strength to search out, with your guidance and wisdom, answers for what I need. Help me to know what I need. Help me to believe that a better life is available for me and completely in your will for me. By faith, I choose to believe.

7

Close Your Eyes, Plug Your Ears, and Sing La-La-La

The Effect of Paralysis

David hated to fly. Moreover, David was terrified of flying. It represented an intolerable situation of being out of control. Not that he'd flown that much, at least growing up. With four kids in the family, flying anywhere wasn't generally an option. Leaving for college was only the second time he'd flown in his life. As a young adult, he'd had to fly back and forth between school and home several times, and each time it had gotten worse. Now even thinking about stuffing himself into that cocoon-like space and hurtling thousands of feet into the air, surrounded by only a thin sheet of metal, was nauseating. He just couldn't do it.

So it was awkward when his boss told his design team one of them would have to fly the following month to make a presentation to a large prospective client in a neighboring state. The four designers all expressed the correct mixture of excitement and anticipation at the prospect, David included. David's excitement and anticipation, though, weren't over the potential business but the potential risk. What if he was asked to go? Would saying no jeopardize his job? How could he get out of it without having to disclose his fear?

And it wasn't just his fear of flying. As David thought about it, he realized he had a similar stomach-sinking feeling about making any sort of high-level presentation. It produced the same kind of out-of-control sense of danger that flying did. This trip was fast becoming his worst nightmare.

Up to this point, David had maneuvered things pretty well to avoid taking such risks. After college, when flying moved from uncomfortable to out of the question, he'd taken a job about a three hours' drive from his parents' house—far enough away to have his own life but close enough that he could drive and not have to fly. Not that he'd accrued that much vacation time, but when he did take a break, it was a weekend trip near his house, to see his parents, or just to stay at home. David liked just staying at home.

So while the others on the team seemed eager to be the one chosen to go, David kept hoping it wouldn't be him. Of course, he could see it from their perspective. Whoever pulled this off would be propelled up the next rung of the company ladder. It would probably mean a promotion and, possibly, a raise. That didn't matter to David; it simply wasn't worth the risk.

Hiding from the Monster

Do you remember ever being terrified at night as a child? Maybe you heard a weird sound you couldn't identify and became frightened. Or maybe you saw a scary show or read a scary book and those images refused to leave you alone as you drifted off to sleep. If you were small enough or fortunate enough, you may have run to your parents' room seeking comfort and relief. However, as you got older, you may have stopped, frozen in fear, sure you were supposed to somehow deal with this yourself. Maybe when you were older, you actually were all alone and there was no one to run to.

Do you remember what it felt like? Your first inclination was to freeze, to stop moving, to listen intently and become very, very quiet. As a child, you may have thought being quiet was the same thing as being invisible. If the monster couldn't hear you, the monster couldn't see you. So you stopped doing anything that might cause the monster to notice. You became paralyzed with fear.

As a child, the monster was a figment of your imagination. A shifting box in the closet became a beast lurking behind the closed door. The cavernous space under your bed became a hiding place for something creepy just waiting to emerge. The scraping branch on the window became a claw on the outside scratching its way inside. These childish fears had a way of dissipating in the light of day as you got older. Adult fears, however, can be harder to banish.

Adults still become paralyzed with fear. While I have seen some people go into that locked-down, motionless state, usually the paralysis appears in their life in other ways. The paralysis—the attempt to hide from the monster—usually takes the form of avoidance or procrastination. When the fear can no longer be contained, it can burst forth in desperate impulsivity. Each behavior starts from the same false premise: that the monster is real.

The monster has many faces, depending on who you are and what you fear. To some, the monster climbs walls, darts quickly, and has eight legs. To others, the monster is a multiheaded beast called a crowd. To David, the monster took the form of an airplane, but it really was any situation he felt powerless to control. Whatever face or form your monster takes, at its core it is your creation. It is a monster with your name on it. It knows what terrifies you most, it understands when you're the most vulnerable, it speaks to you in the language of your fears. It is a reflection of you.

Avoiding the Monster

One of the main strategies used to deal with your anxiety is simply to avoid situations where you might feel anxious. Depending on the source of your anxiety, that may not be so simple. As I've said before, having a specific phobia, like a fear of clowns, for example, is relatively easy to handle. You just never go to the circus or circus-like entertainment. You'll also want to stay away from any movie that has a circus theme and read the back of books to make sure they're safe, avoiding any that have titles like *Under the Big Top* or *Three-Ring Mystery*. If you have children and any of those children are invited to a birthday party, you may want to check with the host family to make sure no one is hiring a clown for the festivities. Depending on the depth of your unease, eating at Jack-in-the-Box could be a stretch. And that's just for something straightforward like clowns. Imagine how difficult it becomes to avoid other, more pervasive things like crowds, speaking to others, heights, or the unknown. Avoidance ceases to become simple; instead, avoidance becomes a complex dance with fear as your partner. The bigger the walls you need for security, the smaller your world becomes.

Monsters also morph. They can be like smoke; you may find a way to dissipate them in one form only to have them coalesce in another. David thought his monster was flying. He thought if he could avoid flying, he could avoid the terror that flying produced. The monster, however, wasn't fear of flying; it was David's fear of being placed in situations where he felt out of control. Flying was his introduction to this deep-seated fear, but that fear began to seep out into other areas. Even though he didn't fly anymore, David was also afraid of speaking to large groups of people and leaving the confines of his "safe" places, like his home, the town he lived in, his parents' house. Within a world of possibilities, David's world shrunk to roughly two hundred square miles.

The awareness of anxiety can be attached to a specific event or situation, but the underlying fear can be more fluid. This is what happens with generalized anxiety disorder or even panic attacks. The fear ends up breaking loose through its own momentum, spilling out and away from the original situation. Now fear is constant and the monster is everywhere.

Forestalling the Monster

When the monster is everywhere and avoiding it is no longer an option, the next strategy is to attempt to forestall it, to put off having to deal with it. You know it's there, you know it's coming; you're just trying to put it off as long as you can.

We are not above using our childhood arsenal to forestall adult fears. One of those childhood strategies is the tendency to duck our heads, close our eyes, plug our ears, and in a sing-song voice yell, "La-la-la-la-la," all in an attempt to obscure something we do not wish to experience. La-la-la-la-la is a tried-and-true form of forestalling the monster. But there are many other ways to forestall the monster.

We have already talked about some of the adult versions of la-la-la-la-la in a previous chapter on self-medicating or self-numbing behaviors. Self-numbing behaviors are all attempts at forestalling the monster. They are meant to create a distraction to allow you to avoid thinking about the monster. They are meant to put it off, to buy time, to allow for some sort of miracle to happen to make the monster go away. Of course, these behaviors never actually make the monster go away. Instead, self-numbing behaviors can become monstrous themselves.

While self-numbing behaviors are meant to forestall the monster by doing something, there is a strategy meant to forestall the monster by doing nothing. It's called procrastination. I have worked with a great number of people who couldn't seem to get anything done. They started projects but had difficulty completing them; the bigger the project, the more the difficulty. When people counted on them the most, it seemed they were the least able to come through. This adversely affected their work, their relationships, and ultimately their sense of self-worth. Unlike some, these people were not suffering from an attention deficit disorder. It wasn't that they couldn't get things done; it's that they were afraid to. When projects were in process only, the monster was at bay. Completion meant risk and vulnerability, for their monster was called failure.

Everyone procrastinates. We put off and avoid things we don't want to do. It takes discipline to move past these tendencies and tackle difficult things. It takes maturity to undertake and complete things that make you uncomfortable. For the anxious and fearful person, difficulty and discomfort are trigger situations. They fear doing something, and so it gets put off. When confronted, they fear even admitting to the fear. It becomes a vicious cycle, with people endlessly making excuses as to why they are putting off doing what they said they'd do. The more they fail to complete their tasks, the harder it is to admit the truth and the greater the temptation to pretend what they are afraid of isn't really there.

Self-numbing behaviors and procrastination are both forestalling techniques that act in complete concert with each other. Self-numbing behaviors drown out the consequences of constantly putting off what needs to be done. When what needs to be done is get help to stop, procrastination shields the self-numbing behavior. The longer the monster is forestalled, the larger it grows.

Fleeing the Monster

Anxious people can appear paralyzed by fear. They can go to extreme lengths to avoid anything that triggers their fear. They can make elaborate excuses and put off handling anything that produces anxiety. All of this creates tremendous tension and pressure. The stress of this pressure creates a tremendous need for relief. Sometimes this pressure is vented through impulsive behavior.

At thirty-three, Carly was anxious all the time. With an eight-year-old son, she felt her youth and whatever beauty she had fading with age. Though she'd tried several relationships since her divorce, nothing was working out. Every day she became more dissatisfied with her job, with her life, and with her prospects. During the past three years, she'd moved four times, never more than ten miles away. She didn't move because she had to but because she kept thinking a new place would somehow make her world seem better. It didn't.

That's when Carly decided the answer was to move to a small town outside Denver. She didn't know anyone there, which somehow made it more attractive. Carly was determined to start her life over, convinced she could find love and happiness in the slower tempo of a small town. So she quit her job, sold all her possessions to pay for the move, yanked her son out of school, and headed off for what she considered greener pastures.

After ten months, when the dreams had washed out along with the temporary jobs she'd been able to find, Carly moved back. It seemed being an unknown in a small town wasn't all it was cracked up to be. Back home at least her family was there and could help take care of her son, who was now more confused and frustrated than ever. When people had politely—and some not so politely—questioned why she'd taken off in the first place, Carly hadn't really been able to explain. It just seemed to make sense at the time. For a time, the sheer upheaval in her life brought on by the move provided effective cover. The move itself overwhelmed the reasons behind it. For a while, Carly felt relief. That time was over, and now she felt worse than ever.

When the stress of anxiety can no longer be avoided, when it can no longer be forestalled, a sense of desperation can set in. You'll find yourself thinking of doing, and sometimes actually doing, things you never thought possible. When being quiet doesn't work, when avoidance doesn't work, you can decide the only alternative is to run. There is something compelling about running; it is a singular pursuit. Running has a way of focusing your attention just on what's ahead instead of what's behind.

I've known people who have run from spouses, parents, and children. They've run from established relationships toward the dream of what if with people they've met online. Like Carly, they've physically moved from place to place, hoping to leave their fears behind. They've run farther and farther down the path toward drug addiction or alcoholism. People run to all sorts of things, but they cannot outrun themselves.

Fears cannot be outrun; they must be faced and overcome. The root of the fears must be understood and put into proper context. Fears cannot stay hidden; they must be forced out into the open, to be examined in the light of truth. Instead of la-la-la-la-la, you need to raise your head, open your eyes, listen, and experience. Because your monster has such power over you, it is imperative you stop avoiding it, putting it off, and running from it and start putting it into its proper perspective.

ANCHORING ACTIVITY

Instead of beginning this exercise with what you fear, I'd like you to start by focusing on what you avoid, what you put off, and what you flee. These are the big things that interrupt your life in major ways and also the little things that complicate your life in small ways.

Think about the situations you find yourself in on a daily basis:

- Do you have an established routine you use every day?
- Does it upset you when that routine is interrupted?
- Are there situations or activities you will go out of your way to avoid?
- What situations or activities make you uncomfortable?

- What activities or situations make you uncomfortable but you do them anyway?

- Has it gotten easier or harder over the past year to engage in those activities or be around those situations?

- In the past year, have you turned down opportunities to try new things because of fear?

- Looking back, do you regret not being able to say yes?

- Do you feel your life would have been enhanced if you'd been able to say yes?

- Are there certain people you specifically avoid because of how they make you feel?

- What are some things you've done to avoid being around those people?

- Have you given up doing something you liked because it would have involved someone you wanted to avoid?

- Do you put off doing certain tasks regularly, like paying the bills or cleaning the house?

- How do you feel when you do them? Name three separate emotions, if possible.

- How do you feel when you put them off? Name three separate emotions, if possible.

- What do you do instead of taking care of those tasks?

- How long are you able to avoid or put off doing unpleasant things?

- In the past two years, what activities have you turned down because you felt afraid?

- What activities have you decided you absolutely will not do and why?

- Do you sometimes wish you could bring yourself to do those things, or are you resigned to never doing them?

- If you could wake up in the morning and have one fear gone, which would it be?
- What would your life be like without that fear?
- What would you be willing to do to have that happen?
- What would you be willing to give up for that to happen?

There are so many things in life to be truly fearful of. So often we neglect those things in order to concentrate on the monsters of our own making, which, perversely, can seem more manageable. So a person so frightened of going to the doctor doesn't, only to be diagnosed with late-stage cancer. A person afraid to fly has a life-threatening car wreck five miles from home. A person terrified of becoming fat, at eighty-two pounds, goes to sleep one night and never wakes up. Our fears are often completely disengaged from the reality of risk. We decide our own dangers, often disregarding what is truly dangerous. We chase after the things that will harm us and run away from the things that can save us. Gaining proper perspective means changing how we think.

Are you ready to do that? Facing your fear means changing who you are, because up to this point you've been willing to live with your fear. You've allowed it to be part of who you are and also to define who you are. You've been trying to manage your fear instead of working toward relieving it altogether. You've allowed your fear to get bigger and your world to get smaller.

Remember, please, that I'm not talking about reasonable fears or reasonable precautions. I'm not talking about the very reasonable fear of sitting on the edge of a ledge overhanging the Grand Canyon. I'm talking about not even going to the Grand Canyon because you have a fear of heights. If you're unwilling to visit the Grand Canyon because of fear, your world is diminished. The more Grand Canyons you avoid, put off, or run from, the more your life is diminished. We were meant to live this life head up with all senses engaged, not huddled in a corner attending to our monsters.

This world is a large and often inhospitable place. In comparison, you and I can seem very small. Small things, by nature, fear larger things. But we are only small in and of ourselves. Remaining small is one option, but another exists. Each of us has been given the option to align ourselves with something bigger, something larger, something greater than ourselves. As a Christian, I choose to align myself with that bigger and greater someone, God and his Son, Jesus Christ.

Paul, in his second letter to Timothy, says, "For God did not give us a spirit of timidity, but a spirit of power, of love and of self-discipline" (1:7). I need these three—power, love, and self-discipline—to banish my own monsters. Power allows me to be stronger than my monsters. Love motivates me to fight them. Self-discipline prepares me for the next battle. These gifts are not mine alone; they are yours also, given by a loving and gracious Father.

Dear God, I take your promise from Deuteronomy 20:4 and claim it as my own: You are the LORD, my God, the one who goes with me, to fight for me against my enemies, to give me victory. Give me victory, O God, over my enemies, including the monsters of my own making. Give me the strength to face my fears and deal with them, knowing you are with me.

PART 2

Experiencing Relief
from Anxiety, Worry, and Fear

8

Relief through Controlling the Volume

What to Turn Up and What to Turn Down

Mandy settled onto the couch, tucking her feet up next to her. As soon as she'd gotten home, she'd changed into her pajamas. She was looking forward to a quiet evening with the house to herself. Don and Brad had left on a "guy" weekend. They'd been fairly vague about their plans, just heading up north to go fishing and whatever else they decided to do. Brad would be entering high school soon, and both seemed to sense that childhood was rapidly ending. Though she'd asked for more details, Mandy had accepted the lack of planning as pretty normal and left it at that.

It was amazing—a whole day and a half to herself. She would put off doing the dishes and sit and watch the kind of movie her guys couldn't stand. The cat seemed more than happy to watch with her. Just before she put on the movie, a news alert flashed across the screen on the local station she'd been watching. There was a pileup on the interstate, three cars involved, with possible fatalities.

Mandy froze. Would the guys have taken the interstate? She started to calculate how long ago they'd left and how many miles they could have traveled. Movie forgotten, Mandy got up, disturbing the cat. Grabbing the phone, she called Don. No answer, so she left a terse message, asking for him to call her back as soon as he got the message. She tried Brad's phone but again no answer. While this was not that unusual, it still filled her with a sense of unease. What was the point of cell phones if people didn't answer?

Irritated now, Mandy decided to watch the movie, telling herself there was nothing to worry about. Thirty minutes into the movie, however, she couldn't stand it any longer and tried both phones again. Nothing. Why hadn't they called her? If they were in that accident, wouldn't at least one of them have been able to call? Unless it was a really bad accident and both were seriously injured. If they were seriously injured, how long would it take the police or hospital to call her? She'd bugged both Don and Brad to enter their home number under "emergency" in their cell phones' address books, but she knew neither of them had. When she'd asked, they'd just rolled their eyes and muttered something noncommittal. They thought she worried too much.

Objectify Your Thoughts

In the last chapter, we talked about worry and anxiety taking the form of a monster. These emotions can truly take on a life of their own. But the life of that monster is powered by you. Your thoughts feed the monster. You hate the monster but are very attached to your thoughts. They incubate in your brain and, upon release, find a swift and smooth transition from unconscious to conscious. Your own thoughts *seem* right to you because they arise out of you.

But what if your thoughts aren't correct? What if they aren't really even the truth? Thoughts are not events. They are not objective; they are subjective. In the world of anxiety, there is a vast difference between the objective and the subjective. Objective means something most people would agree upon. Merriam-Webster's dictionary defines the word *objective* as being "in the realm of sensible experience independent of individual thought and perceptible by all observers: having reality independent of the mind."[1] Objective things have a reality independent of the mind because the mind can, sometimes, really mess things up. Subjective is the opposite of objective. The word *subjective* means "characteristic of or belonging to reality as perceived rather than as independent of mind."[2]

So there is a reality to what happens that is independent of what you think about it. For many people, this is a foreign concept. Truth, to them, consists of their impressions, thoughts, opinions, biases, feelings, and assumptions. *I think, therefore it is.* Subjective thoughts are perfectly suited to feed the monster. The thoughts are yours; the monster is yours. The subjective thoughts you feed your monster are tailor-made to strengthen it.

This is not easy for some people to accept. Their subjective perceptions are so strong that they drown out objective reality. These people live within a world of delusion where what they think will happen will, what they think is happening is, what they think did happen did, even if all evidence points to the contrary. It is a world where the subjective crowds out the objective. It is a world of monsters and terrors and things that go bump in the night. Now, granted, not everyone with anxiety goes to this extreme. There are some people who actually believe false things are true; we call them delusional and obsessive thinkers. There are other people who merely *fear* that false things are true; we call them anxious, worried, concerned, overwrought, and stressed.

Because your thoughts are so well suited to feeding your fears, it's very important to begin to objectify your thoughts, to get them more in line with what is true instead of mired down in your perceptions. Again, this isn't easy; people cling to the perceived truth

121

of their thoughts tenaciously. It takes courage to examine them and strength to change them.

Let's take Mandy's example and compare the truth of the situation to her perception. After hearing on the news about the freeway pileup, Mandy became anxious about the well-being of her husband and son. What did Mandy think and what did Mandy actually know? Let's start with the latter and look at it from different directions:

- Mandy knew there was an accident involving several vehicles that occurred north of her on the interstate.
- Mandy knew her husband and son were headed "up north" to go fishing.
- Mandy did not know if, in fact, her husband and son were going to use the interstate to get up north.
- Mandy did not know if her husband and son were involved in the accident.

So Mandy knew two things and didn't know two things. For anxious people, what they don't know outweighs what they do know. For anxious people, when what they don't know concerns something they fear, a vacuum is created—a vacuum of information. When this vacuum of information exists, anxious people will fill it with the content of their own perceptions. Because their perceptions are negative and fearful, so is their emerging sense of reality. This is what happened to Mandy and led to her increasing anxiety.

When neither Don nor Brad was reachable by his cell phone on two separate occasions, half an hour apart, Mandy's perceptions of the situation, based on her fears, began to take over. She became increasingly worried that they'd been involved in the accident and hadn't called because they were injured and couldn't.

However, just before running headlong into full-blown panic, Mandy stopped and took a moment to think through her conclusions. She knew Don and Brad were headed "up north," but she really didn't know where that was or if it even required taking the interstate. The possibility existed, but in her panic, she'd turned that possibility into certainty. But was it really certain Don and Brad were in that accident? Mandy quieted her fears and stopped to calculate the odds.

When anxiety and panic set in, it's helpful to stop and intentionally calculate the odds of what you fear. Fear lends certainty to even the most far-fetched possibility. How many people die every year of snake or spider bites? The number is astronomically small, yet people live daily with a fear of both. Of the many people who fly every year, how many actually die in plane crashes? Again, the number is extremely small, yet a fear of flying affects a large number of people. As I said before, it's more dangerous to drive to the store for ice cream than to fly halfway around the world. Subjective thoughts tell you to be fearful of flying, but the truth is you're more likely to be killed getting to the airport than flying on the plane.

When Mandy stopped to calculate the odds of her husband and son being on that road, at that time, at that exact location, she realized the odds were very small. They were probably so preoccupied with what they were doing that they just didn't answer their phones. With a twinge of irritation, Mandy realized they were out having a great time, and she was wasting this precious opportunity for a little alone time by needlessly worrying. Rewinding her movie, she went back to the opening credits and started over.

About halfway through, Don called. They actually had taken the interstate but were several miles south of the accident. The freeway, of course, was completely backed up, so they'd decided to get off and see a movie while traffic cleared. Their cell phones had been on silent, so they hadn't known she'd called. As soon as they got out, Brad turned on his phone, saw her call, and alerted Don. Don, realizing she'd been concerned, told her exactly where they were going from that point on and promised to phone when they arrived.

In the midst of feeling anxious, it can be difficult to think objectively, but it is extremely important. If you're fearful of flying or snakes or spiders, you can always look up the statistical odds of injury or death. Depending on what you fear, however, there may not be any statistics. If you're worried about something like losing your job, you're going to need to think back over the course of your own life to find the data. For example, how many jobs have you had and how many jobs have you lost? If you have lost jobs in the past, are conditions now the same as they were then? If you're worried about something like being humiliated in public, consider how many times you've been in a public situation versus how many times you've actually been humiliated. (Think about how many times you've actually, objectively, been humiliated and not how many times you worried about being humiliated or felt humiliated. You need to objectively calculate the odds.)

Fear establishes a toehold in your mind, then infiltrates your thoughts, establishing a stronghold in your mind, leading to a stranglehold over your life. Depending on your level of anxiety, you may not be able to work through these calculations on your own. You may need to discuss these issues with a professional counselor, someone trained to walk you through this process and help you separate objective knowledge from your subjective perceptions. If that's the case, don't feel bad about it. All of us have issues we have difficulty seeing in our lives because we're so close to them. It's why talking things over with trusted family members or friends is invaluable. The important thing, if you aren't able to work through this on your own, is to ask for help. Anxieties breed in secret. Hidden fears intensify. Place your fears outside yourself and you'll be amazed at how quickly they are reduced to actual size.

Facing the Monster

So you start out by asking, "What are the facts?" Separate objective knowledge from subjective perceptions. These are the facts that exist outside your mind and your fears. They are the facts that are evident and visible to others. This is the reality that exists outside your mind. If it is difficult for you to determine what that objective reality is, again, ask for help.

Next, based on that objective knowledge, ask yourself, "What are the odds?" If what you fear involves a universal danger, like flying or water or lightning or snakes, find out what the actual odds are of being harmed or killed. If it's something specific to you, review the past, and look for objective outcomes—what actually happened instead of what you feared would happen.

There is a third step if the first two fail to stem the tide of anxiety. Sometimes the most stubborn fears are wedged in your mind because you've looked at the facts, calculated the odds, and decided that, even though the odds are small, the size of the fear outweighs the size of the odds. Big fears have a way of trumping small odds in the realm of anxiety. So to help with this, ask yourself, "If this is true, what can I do?"

People often lament, "But what if" and use this unknown as a reason to continue living their lives paralyzed with fear. An effective way to move them past this stage is to help them see what life looks like at the other end of what if. The way to do this is through the third step, to turn their what if into an if what. For some fears, you may need to ask, "Okay, *if* this were to happen, *what* would it mean and *what* would I do?" (Again, depending on the nature of your fears and the level of your anxiety, consider working through this with a counselor or even a trusted friend or loved one.)

Taming the monster of what if sometimes takes the deeper examination of if what. If the worst you can imagine were to happen, what would that mean? How would your life go on? What would you do? What would your life be like? You need to know there is life at the other end of your fears, even your greatest ones. You need to know you have resources and help available, even if the worst thing were to happen.

For some people, the worst thing that can happen is their own illness or death or the illness or death of a loved one. Calculating the odds for this leads to a stark conclusion: people can become sick, and everyone will eventually die. Because so many people fear these two outcomes, they shy away from actually thinking through what this would mean. It is a meaningful and worthwhile exercise to think about and determine how you would handle sickness and how you will deal with death—your own or that of a loved one.

But what if your fear isn't about death or dying? What if you are terrified of speaking in front of a crowd or losing your job? This third step is still very valuable. If you were called on to speak in front of a crowd and you forgot what you were supposed to say, what would you do? I like to have people come up with three concrete actions they could take to help in that dreaded situation. One man I worked with had a paralyzing fear of public speaking. I said to him, "Okay, if you had to speak in front of others, what would you do?" After thinking about it for a while he said, "If I absolutely had to, I'd have either my wife or my buddy at work right there with me. Also, I'd write down beforehand what I wanted to say and just read it out loud. If that was too hard, I'd have my wife or my friend read it for me." We also talked about how, if that ever were to happen, he could make mention of how difficult speaking in front of others was for him and ask for some understanding from the people listening. So many other people share that fear. I told him there'd probably be quite a few heads nodding if he mentioned it; he wouldn't be alone.

Another person I worked with lived in fear of losing her job. "Okay," I said, "if you lost your job, what would you do?" At first, all she could talk about was the panic she'd feel, but I gently pressed her to think about three positive things she could *do* and not become stuck on what she'd *feel*. She couldn't think of anything right away, but then, after she'd expressed her anxiety, she laughed a little and said she could take a break. She admitted she spent so much time worrying about losing her job that she rarely enjoyed it. She was fearful of letting it go, even during days off or vacations. She had to admit that, if she ever did lose her job, she'd actually be able to rest. Upon further prompting, she said she'd take some time off for herself. After that, she'd start looking again, maybe for something completely different, something less stressful. "So," I commented, "losing your job wouldn't really be the end of the world. It would be the end of that job, but it might just be the beginning of something better."

Living Past, Future, but Never Present

The voice of fear never lets you simply live today, for today. It always seems to harass you, dredging up things of the past while tormenting you with disasters of the future. When it takes over, you're caught in a temporal vise, with the problems of the past and the fears of the future crushing the truth of today. You never seem to be able to live in the moment, enjoying and experiencing what is happening now. Instead, you're consumed with what happened in the past and terrified of what will happen in the future.

People need to keep their thoughts in the present instead of letting them go off in all directions, where they can find some worry to latch on to. This is especially true of anxious people, who often complain of runaway thoughts, feeling as if their mind has been hijacked on a terrifying ride of negativity and dread.

What to Turn Down and What to Turn Up

Negative, pessimistic thoughts drag you down. They pollute your mind and your thoughts. They weaken you and strengthen your fears. Even when you're aware of them, it can take practice and diligence to get rid of them entirely. In the interim, you may need to admit to hearing them but then intentionally turn down their volume. It's as if you say, "Yes, I hear you, but I choose not to react to you. The action I choose to take in response is to tune you out."

For some people, this negative sound track has the banal blandness of an infomercial. For others, their negative sound track is voiced by someone they know or knew. It can be a parent, a sibling, a spouse, a teacher. The sound track can be seemingly endless or made up of a single, cutting remark. This sound track is the source of so many of your perceptions or, better, misperceptions. This is the voice your fears, anxieties, insecurities, worries, and concerns take. This is the shrill voice of escalation that demands your attention. Allow it to gain your attention, but not so it can gain control over you. Acknowledge it so you can claim control over it. Reclaim your thoughts. When they scream negativity, pessimism, doom, and despair, make a choice to turn them down. Say to yourself, "I hear you, but you're wrong."

Often, it's not enough just to turn down the volume on the negative. You must also turn up the volume on the positive. It's like hearing a song you don't like on the radio and deciding to change the channel. You need to change the channel from negative to positive.

Say to yourself, "I hear you, but you're wrong; I *am* a worthwhile person."

Say to yourself, "I hear you, but you're wrong; I *have* amounted to something."

Say to yourself, "I hear you, but you're wrong; I *don't have* to be perfect to be loved."

Say to yourself, "I hear you, but you're wrong; I *don't have* to be in control to be safe."

Say to yourself, "I hear you, but you're wrong; I *am* strong enough to face today and I *am* strong enough to face tomorrow."

If the sound track of your life is full of negativity, you need to start writing a new one. You need to look for and celebrate the positives in your life. You need to change the channel from pessimism to optimism. At first, this will seem strange and stilted. It won't be natural for you. But you need to start looking at the glass of your life as half full, not half empty. You need to begin to concentrate on and really incorporate the positive things that happen to you. You need to appreciate and dwell on the good, including the good in you and around you. Looking through the eyes of fear, you miss so much of the beauty and hope in the world. Listening to the voice of fear, you dismiss so much of the beauty and hope in the world. It's time to change your channel.

ANCHORING ACTIVITY

By now you're very familiar with the voice of your fear. It's been loud; it's been constant; it's been overwhelming. It's time to start cultivating and listening to a softer voice, a smaller voice: the voice of hope. The voice of fear appears to be the voice of power, but that is a sham. Over time, fear does not produce power; it only drains it. Hope is the true voice of power. Hope enables you to see beyond your perceptions to the horizon of a new dawn. Fear says everything will end; hope says life will go on.

I firmly believe in the power of optimism, hope, and joy. Optimism is the default setting that looks for the good. Hope is the firm belief that the good does exist. And joy celebrates that existence. There is great good all around you, and it's time you started looking for it. Begin the process by filling in the following blanks.

The Good about Me and Who I Am

1.

2.

3.

4.

5.

The Good in My Life Right Now

1.

2.

3.

4.

5.

The Good in My Life in the Past

1.

2.

3.

4.

5.

The Good in My Life in the Future

1.

2.

3.

4.

5.

Why I Choose Hope over Fear

1.

2.

3.

4.

5.

Why I Choose to Live in the Moment Today

1.

2.

3.

4.

5.

The world is quite effective at recording the negative sound track for your life. There is a seemingly endless supply of problems, troubles, fears, worries, concerns, and anxieties. If that is all you listen to, it will be difficult for you to switch to a good channel. I can think of no better source for material for your good channel than something called the Good Book. I'm speaking, of course, of the Bible. In Luke 18:19, Jesus says that God is good, and I believe it. I have experienced it in my own life and in the lives of so many others, whether believers in God or not. God is good and wants good for you. He plans for good while knowing that your life will not always be smooth and that, sometimes, you'll simply be overwhelmed.

When I am overwhelmed by life, I take heart in the story of Jeremiah. The theme verse for the Center comes from Jeremiah 29:11: "'For I know the plans I have for you,' declares the LORD, 'plans to prosper you and not to harm you, plans to give you hope and a future.'" Here is another passage that reminds me, even in the pits I find myself in, I am not alone: "The waters closed over my head, and I thought I was about to be cut off. I called on your name, O LORD, from the depths of the pit. You heard my plea: 'Do not close your ears to my cry for relief.' You came near when I called you, and you said, 'Do not fear.' O Lord, you took up my case; you redeemed my life" (Lam. 3:54–58).

When you feel like you're in over your head and you're about to be cut off, God says, "Do not fear." Concentrate on the good; listen to God. Allow his words to fill your soul and give you hope.

Dear Father, may your voice of hope be stronger than the voices of despair. Give me the strength to wait and listen for you to speak and not give the world the last word on my life. Teach me your words and your ways; make my thoughts your thoughts. Help me to have faith. Give me stamina to practice these things until your voice is all I hear.

9

Relief through Refusing to Sweat

Say No to the Small Stuff

⎯⎯⎯⎯⎯⎯⎯⎯

Stretching after sitting still far too long, Craig was about to log off his computer at work when he got an email alert. Frowning and looking at the time, Craig opened his inbox and accessed the new message from his supervisor. With a groan, he read that he had just been assigned a report due by the end of the week. Sighing, Craig could feel his stomach react with stress and resentment. As if he didn't have enough to do already! Craig imagined his blood pressure was starting to spike. There simply weren't enough hours in the day to get everything done, and now this too. Didn't anybody care about him and how he was feeling? Couldn't they see the sort of stress this placed on him? Where a minute ago he'd just been tired, now he was tired, angry, and worried. He had no idea how he was going to get everything done. If he didn't get this latest project done, his supervisor would be mad. If he worked late too many nights, his wife would be mad. If he had to renege on something with the kids because of this, his kids would be mad. Everybody was allowed to be mad but him. He was just supposed to suck it up and somehow get it all done. It was unfair.

As he made his way home, Craig wasn't really concentrating on driving; he was on autopilot as he fumed and complained. It wasn't just work that was piling up on him. He thought of the three evening meetings he had to go to over the next two weeks. Then there was the birthday party for his wife's brother on Saturday and Sarah's soccer game on Sunday. Naturally, that one was forty-five minutes away.

By the time he drove into the garage, Craig was almost nauseous, worrying about all the things—the tasks, the duties, the responsibilities, the activities—that threatened to suffocate his life. He never had any time for himself, for doing the things he wanted. It was always about taking care of things for everyone else. Sometimes he just wanted to run away, but there really wasn't anywhere to go.

The family seemed to sense his mood and left him alone for the evening, but being alone with his thoughts wasn't the best place for Craig. By the time he dragged himself to bed, after mindlessly watching television for too long into the night, he could feel the dread of another panic attack waiting in the wings. His breathing was too shallow, his mind too agitated, his heart too loud. He felt like the weight of the world was threatening to crash down on him, and he didn't know how he was going to handle it all. If one more person asked him for one more thing, he thought he'd explode. At this point, he wasn't sure if that would be bad or good.

It's said that misery loves company. I would add that anxiety loves company too. Worries are happiest in a crowd, and fears flock together. There is something about the critical mass generated by a piling on of concerns that makes objectivity difficult to discover. When too many worries are blaring in ear-splitting volume, peace is drowned out. When the body is jacked up on too many stresses, the path to relaxation is obliterated. When you're in a full-blown panic, there is no such thing as "small stuff." All stuff is big.

When Small Stuff Is Big

No matter how much we would like it to be different, there are only so many hours in a day. We are finite creatures with a finite amount of time to get things done. We don't have a choice about how much time there is in each day, but we do have a choice about what we spend that time on. Our choices indicate our values. But just as we have trouble accurately assessing true risk, we also have trouble accurately assessing true value. We spend our time afraid of what won't harm us while oblivious to what will. We spend our time consumed with the urgent while neglecting the important. Anxieties make it difficult to recognize what is truly dangerous and appreciate what is worthwhile.

This condition of constantly submitting to the urgent while neglecting the important has been called the tyranny of the urgent. Anxieties are nothing if not urgent. Once anxiety has established its own urgency, all things are filtered through this sense of panic and chaos. Any objectivity is jettisoned in the desperation of the moment, which is anything but momentary. In this condition, it's impossible not to sweat because everything becomes urgent and there is no small stuff. Welcome to the black-and-white world of anxiety. It is a world awash in worries and sweat.

In the last chapter, we talked about turning down the volume on the negative in your life and turning up the volume on the positive. One of the most important ways to do this is to recognize that your life actually consists of small stuff. In fact, a good portion of what you experience negatively every day really is just small stuff; it's just life happening as it does. It may seem perpetual, but it isn't personal.

Do you remember in chapter 2 when we talked about the effect of thought-life, hidden assumptions, and mistaken beliefs? We talked about the tendency of anxious people to personalize everything. It's the tendency to make everything that happens all about you. When everything that happens is all about you, you step into a world of self-absorption. When everything that happens is perceived as negative, you live your life in a state of siege. When you are under attack, everything is urgent, everything is relevant, nothing is safe. Everything feels like a personal attack, even small stuff. In this black-and-white world, urgency is a way of life because your life is seen as constantly under attack.

When you live like this, neutrality doesn't exist. Any imposition, mistake, requirement, obligation—whether agreed to or not—feels like one more attack. Enemies are everywhere, and the only person you can trust is yourself. This, of course, isn't true, but anxiety has a way of resetting your reality gauge. What you feel supersedes what you know. No one else understands; no one else helps. It's an odd paradox that, while anxieties love company, they like it best when you are isolated.

Learning to Let Go

Anxieties scream that you're in danger. Every action taken, every word spoken is filtered through this position of being under attack. This state of hypersensitivity is brought on by the physical and emotional charge of anxiety. Everyone is either friend or foe. Under this anxiety alert, there is no random occurrence, no casual comment, and no mild inconvenience. Again, this is a black-and-white world of absolutes.

The important thing to remember is that this world exists only in your mind. It is not a true reflection of the circumstances of your life. As difficult as it is, as risky as it seems, you need to stand down from this red alert, drop your weapon of black-and-white thinking, and surrender to the truth. Everyone is not out to get you; there are people who do understand; not everything that happens to you is personal; just because something feels urgent doesn't mean it really is.

Simply put, you need to learn to let go. Anxious people not only hang on to a great many things but also constantly grab on to new ones in order to control their anxiety. They believe controlling things will bring them safety, but doing so only leads to a greater sense of risk. The more things they seek to control, the more things they are called to defend. The more things they are called to defend, the more it appears they are being attacked. The more it appears they are being attacked, the more things they seek to control. The answer in all this lies with the beginning of the spiral: seek fewer things to control, or, in other words, let more stuff go. Letting things go in order to gain peace seems like a reasonable trade-off. I will warn you, however, that anxieties are anything but reasonable and simplifying your life may not be as simple as it sounds.

One of the main strategies to reduce your anxiety level is to de-clutter your life. Clutter in your life is very much like clutter in your house. I can't think of a better word for it. Clutter is all that stuff you hang on to because you think it is or might be important. It's stuff you mean to take care of but haven't yet. It's stuff you're willing to let take up space while you decide what to do with it. It's like hoarding activities even though they make your life miserable. The more of this stuff you pack into your life, the less time you have and the more stress you feel. The more stress you feel, the stronger your anxieties grow.

The first step to simplifying your life is to examine what you're doing and start doing less. How do you feel about that last sentence? Does it make you anxious just thinking about doing less? Are you worried that you'll choose the wrong thing, that you'll make a mistake and drop something urgent? Are you arguing with me, even now, countering that you'd love to give something up but you just can't, that everything you're doing is important?

If so, take a deep breath and calm down. Those are your anxieties talking. They've hijacked your brain and are in full defense mode. They're not speaking from the truth; they're speaking from their false perceptions. Before you are ready to get rid of the clutter in your life, you need to get rid of the clutter in your thoughts. This isn't something that will come naturally to you; quite the opposite. You're going to need to wrest control of your mind back from your anxieties. You're going to need to value your peace of mind, your sense of self, and truth more than you value your anxieties. You may think you don't value your anxieties, that all you want to do is get rid of them, but consider something for a moment. We tend to hold on to the things we value. If you didn't really value your anxieties on some level, you wouldn't have held on to them this long.

Are you an anxiety hoarder? I'm not talking about being merely a collector of fears but rather a hoarder. Hoarded things do not produce pleasure. To the hoarder, they are seen as protection. They do not produce a positive; they protect against a negative. There is a genuine fear of failing to have or throwing these hoarded things out, for being without these things means being in danger.

I'd like you to think about whether you are as attached to your anxious thoughts as a hoarder is attached to things. A hoarder has a tremendously difficult time letting things go and feels extremely unsafe when doing so. Maybe it's difficult for you to see how beautiful your life really is because it's become cluttered and obscured with all your anxieties. Maybe it's difficult for you to really live your life because you have to spend so much time maneuvering around your worries and fears. Have you had enough? Are you ready to jettison your anxieties and de-clutter your life?

ANCHORING ACTIVITY

How you spend your time tells a great deal about what you value. So for this chapter's activity, I'd like you to keep track. I'd like you to track how you spend your time in a couple of ways. First, think about your typical monthly activities. For a thirty-day month, write down how many hours you spend sleeping, working, getting to work, taking care of household chores, fulfilling family obligations, etc.

Next, think about what you do with your "discretionary" time and just how much time that actually is. For example, during a twenty-four-hour day, most people spend a third of the time sleeping, a third of the time working (for most days), leaving a third of the time. I'd like you to monitor what you do with that other third—that discretionary time. Ask yourself some questions:

- How much time do I really have for myself?
- Which activities are ones that I have deemed important?
- Which activities are those other people have required me to do?
- For each of the activities listed, decide whether you like doing it. Is it an activity that brings you pleasure? Why? What do you value about the activity?
- For each activity listed, think about stopping it tomorrow. What is your immediate reaction? Can you see yourself in the future not doing this activity? Does the thought of stopping this activity make you anxious? If so, why?
- Are there any activities you would like to give up but don't feel you can? Which ones? Why do you feel obligated or compelled to continue doing them? What do you think would happen if you stopped?
- As you looked over your list, were you surprised at how much or how little time you're actually spending in a given area? If so, which ones and why?

Here are a couple of other things to watch for when tracking how you spend your time. Watch to see how much time you actually spend sleeping. Watch also how much time you spend working. Work is an enormous source of anxiety for many people. Work causes anxiety, and it can also be used as a way to relieve anxiety.

It can be startling to see how you really spend your time. Think about what this says about your anxieties and your priorities. You may, for example, believe that you value your relationship with your family. However, when you look at your tracking, you may discover that you spend much more time watching television than you spend with your children. You may find that you spend much more time on the computer than you do with your spouse. You may say that you value spending time with friends but realize you actually spend very little time every month in contact with other people. Evaluate honestly why you spend time doing what you do. What is the positive outcome you expect from spending this time? What is the negative consequence you seek to avoid from spending this time? As you look at each activity, determine if you use it as a way to manage or deflect an anxiety and which one.

As you look over your activities, determine if any have such a net negative consequence in your life that it makes sense to give it up. Notice I said *net negative*. Some activities you enjoy that have positive aspects can also come with negative ones. Relaxing and watching television can be a positive, but if you are spending hours every evening doing that, to the detriment of your existing relationships or obligations, this activity has a net negative effect. Keeping a clean and orderly home is a definite positive, but if you hold the rest of your family hostage while you insist on absolute order to keep your anxiety at bay, this is a net negative. Working is a necessity for most of us, but if your job is overtaking all the other areas of your life, including the people you love, it is a net negative. Working is a necessity, but the job you have may not be.

It is important for you to know why you do what you do and the value you place on it. You need to be able to examine on a regular basis the activities that make up your life and make changes as needed. You must be in charge of that decision—you and not your anxieties. Most of us, me included, allow too many activities to crowd our days. It's important to evaluate periodically whether each activity is still valuable and worthwhile.

Anxieties have a way of lying to us about what is valuable and what is not. If you find you're confused and need some guidance breaking out of anxiety's black-and-white world, if you find you're having difficulty letting go out of fear, allow me to recommend an excellent book. A long time ago a man delved into a black-and-white world where every action was urgent and critical, where every undertaking was monumental, with monumental ramifications and monumental consequences. It was a world where every single thing was so important that it turned out nothing was. The man declared it all "meaningless, a chasing after the wind." His name was Solomon, and he wrote a collection of truths based on his experience called the book of Proverbs. Living a life based on the world he called folly. Living a life based on God he called wisdom. Solomon found that most of the things people strive for are meaningless and don't deliver as promised. He found that people often fear the wrong things and fail to fear the right things. As you seek to understand what is real and what is not, what is truth and what is not, what is valuable and what is not, Proverbs is a worthwhile read.

This brings up another point. How much time do you devote each month to God? How much do your activities reflect a devotion to him, and how much do they reflect a devotion to your anxieties? Scripture says that God's name is Jealous (Exod. 34:14). If you have placed your anxieties, like an idol, before God, it is his will that you return completely to him. He desires you to trust him, to rely on him to provide you with security and peace, with safety and refuge. Anxieties are negative drainers; God is an abundant provider. Work to lay your anxieties down, one by one, before God. Then fill the time and redirect the energy you used in worry and fear by drawing closer to God. Allow his might and his presence to crowd out your fears and doubts.

I confess, Father, that I have been living a meaningless
life, concerned and worried about all the wrong things.

141

I confess I have relied on my fears and worries to direct my steps and my thoughts instead of turning to you. They have become so much a part of who I am. I need help to separate myself from them. Help me to see and understand why I do the things I do. Give me courage to listen to your voice and make changes. Help me to simplify my life so that I can devote myself to the things that really matter. I want to live a meaningful life for you. Show me what a meaningful life is and then help me change my life to reflect it.

10

Relief through Learning to Relax

How to Work at Not Working

"I don't know why I even bothered to ask," Teresa's husband told her, an exasperated sigh escaping in frustration. Without another word, he began to gather up the various bats, balls, and gloves, yelling for the kids to get in the car. They were all headed out for a Saturday morning at the park and then lunch at Denny's. The kids were giggly and excited. Each of them said good-bye to Teresa on their way out the door, with the youngest giving her a hug—just a hug. Even the littlest one knew better than to ask if she would go with them. It was always a no camouflaged in a regretful-sounding "I can't."

With a weak smile and wave, Teresa closed the door, resentment instantly flaring. Sure, they had all the time in the world to go out and play, while she never did. There was always something else to be done around the house. Saturdays were work days, not play days, at least for her. Someone had to be responsible.

It was barely ten in the morning, and already Teresa could feel the stress of the day. Her list was long, as usual. At least the rest of the family would be gone for hours and out of her way. She could get done what she needed without them trailing behind, messing up whatever she did. For a brief span of time, Teresa could have things the way she wanted them. She experienced such a sense of relief when everything was done—and that was the problem. Things were never done, at least not permanently. She'd fix something, but it wouldn't stay that way.

Teresa had briefly considered going when her husband had brought up his plan for today. He'd been excited about getting out for the first really nice weekend of the year. She might have thought about it longer if the house hadn't been such a wreck. Things had been bothering her for several weeks now, things she hadn't been able to get to, and she had just reached a point where she couldn't stand it any longer. This stuff had to get done, no matter what else was going on.

When she'd tried to explain this to Mike, he'd gotten upset and remarked that she never seemed to be able to just stop and relax. Snapping back at him, she'd retorted that she'd relax when the work was done, unlike some people. Teresa had been ready for a full-on fight, but Mike had simply breathed in really deep and walked out of their bedroom. Tense and on edge, Teresa stayed behind to straighten.

This chapter is about *learning* to relax, because I've found that this isn't a skill of the anxious. Relaxation is a state of mind and body, and it is a skill that anxious people need to learn. Some people come by this skill naturally. They're the people who can sit at a bus stop and just look at the scenery without stressing over the timing of the next bus. They're the people who have the uncanny ability to fall asleep on an airplane in a semivertical position surrounded by total strangers. They're the people who just smile when they learn about a delay and seem perfectly happy to go amuse themselves until whatever it is finally happens. Anxious people sometimes consider these people slow and unmotivated, as if their lives and activities are somehow less important than theirs. Anxious people often treat these people dismissively while at the same time look at them enviously. Anxious people wonder, *How do they do that?* What they really mean is, *How can I do that?*

Give Yourself Permission

Have you ever watched a military company executing a parade drill? All of the soldiers advance in lockstep with rigid bodies and precise movements. Or have you seen a company of soldiers standing ramrod straight in full salute? It can be quite impressive. There comes a point, however, when this position begins to look a bit uncomfortable. The longer it goes on, the more you think, *How long do they have to stay that way?* It can be a relief to hear the leader of the company say, "At ease," releasing the soldiers from such a tense posture. Anxious people spend a great deal of their lives at attention with their fears and concerns in full control. When fears and concerns have control, they rarely allow you to live any part of your life "at ease."

To learn to relax, you need to first give yourself permission to do so. This tends to be difficult for anxious people, who often don't believe they can. In response to the question, "Why don't you relax?" they say, "I can't." They will then proceed to give a long list of impassioned reasons why it is impossible for them to relax. They believe they are not in charge of whether or not they can relax. Instead, they feel compelled by circumstances to be constantly at attention, watching for the anticipated disaster, discomfort, irritation, source of anger, frustration, worry, or fear. They believe they can never stand down from this attitude of alert. This is what happens when fear is given charge of your life. One of the biggest breakthroughs in working with anxiety is recognizing that "I can't" is really "I won't."

Fear and anxieties say you're able to relax only when you're safe, with safety defined not by circumstances but by feelings. Safety means feeling safe, not *being* safe. Since fears and anxieties never allow you to feel safe, there's never a time when you feel you can relax.

This isn't really true, however. Relaxation is something that can be experienced regardless of circumstances. Think about natural childbirth. One of the largest components to this is intentional, directed relaxation. Instead of fighting the contraction, the woman is counseled to respond to the pain by intentionally relaxing her body. This allows her to move through the contraction in a relaxed state, reducing her reaction to the pain. Relaxation is also used in pain management, especially in situations of chronic pain. Learning to relax, even in the face of pain, allows your body to be in a better position to manage the stress of the pain. This relaxation is counterintuitive but, nonetheless, effective.

Fears and anxieties are painful. When the body is stressed—either through a reaction to pain or a reaction to fear—breathing is rapid and shallow, the heart races, stress hormones release, and muscles tighten. Intentional relaxation counters each of these. Relaxation returns the body to a normal pattern of breathing, heart rate and blood pressure drop, endorphins are released instead of stress hormones, and muscles relax. Intentional relaxation allows you to take control of your own body and its systems, instead of having those systems hijacked by stress and fear. Relaxation allows you to experience inner calm.

To learn to relax, you need to take back charge of your own life. That's the only way you'll be able to create a place in your life for relaxation. You need to be in charge in order to assign relaxation its proper value and priority in your life. You need to start saying no to fear and yes to relaxation. You need to stop listening to all the reasons why you can't and start expressing all the reasons why you can and should. Saying yes to inner calm isn't something that can be accomplished in a single, declarative statement. You must continually remind yourself to enter this state of calm and sometimes fight to stay there. With each visit, you work toward staying longer and calmer each time.

For those of you who are perfectionists, this will be especially difficult. You've probably created a complex structure in your life that addresses your fears but leaves little room for relaxation. Because perfection is impossible to achieve on the inside, perfectionists are consumed with things on the outside, with controlling their own environment and bending it in ways that simulate a situation of safety.

This was Teresa. Because she lived a life controlled by her fears, worries, and concerns, which constantly battled inside her, she compensated through rigidly controlling her outside world. She was, in the words of some, a neat freak. Everything in her home, her car, her workplace had to be in order and in place. There was nothing she liked better than going into new homes and seeing the perfect, staged environments. It didn't matter to her that real people didn't live there. She dreamt of living in houses like these and worked day after day in a futile attempt to achieve that illusion, all in a house with a husband, three kids, a dog, and a goldfish, with a garbage disposal that leaked, weeds that grew in the yard, and a neighbor whose weeds were worse. Teresa would give herself permission to relax only when she considered everything around her "perfect." It never was, so she never relaxed.

Some anxious people are, paradoxically, opposite of those like Teresa. While Teresa coped with her fears and worries by "doing," some anxious people do the opposite. Teresa sprang into action in order to quell her fears. Some people literally go into shut-down mode. Instead of doing everything, they do nothing. This state of doing nothing, however, is not a relaxed state. It is a numbed, gray state where inactivity is seen as a refuge from fear. Thinking about and doing nothing is meant to keep the monsters at bay. Relaxation is not numbness. The first is an active, engaged state of rest and rejuvenation. The second is a rejection of the first. Numbness isn't interested in feeling anything, not even relaxed.

The more stressed and anxious you are, the weirder learning to relax is going to feel. But it's only weird because you're unfamiliar with it. It's like any new skill. At first it seems awkward and unnatural. Give yourself permission to be uncomfortable with it, but do it anyway. The more you practice relaxation, the more accustomed you'll become to it and the easier being at ease will be.

Learning to Relax

We've already gone over the first step to learning to relax, which is to give yourself permission to do so. You may need to provide your own reassurance that nothing bad will happen to you if you relax. You may need to allow yourself the "reward" of relaxation even if you haven't done all the things you think you should have done. If you've denied yourself the right to relax, you may need to start slowly. Start with granting yourself permission to try one of the following relaxation suggestions. I'd start with the first because it's the most fundamental and do it at least once a day. For the others, you'll want to try one of these at least once a week.

Because you're learning, begin by choosing a day of the week to start that is less stressful than others. Don't add to an already stressful day by taking on another task. At first, this relaxation exercise is going to seem just like something you "have" to do, but that's okay; you're learning. Once you're more comfortable with your intentional times of relaxation, you can move toward incorporating them into your more stressful days.

Controlled breathing. Often, during times of anxiety and certainly during panic attacks, your breathing can deviate from its natural patterns. Breathing is meant to accommodate and balance our need for oxygen. When anxiety hits, many people hyperventilate. This means they take in more oxygen than their body needs. This throws off the balance between oxygen and carbon dioxide in the body. When you get too much oxygen, your pulse speeds up, you feel dizzy and disconnected, and you experience tingling in your face, hands, or feet. Becoming over-oxygenated can even make you feel like you're suffocating, causing you to breathe even faster. Continue hyperventilating and you can even pass out, which is your body's way of returning its breathing to a more normal pattern and restoring the proper balance between oxygen and carbon dioxide in your bloodstream.

During anxiety and panic, your breathing can seem like a runaway freight train clacking down the track out of control. That is why it is important for you to learn how to take back control of your breathing and return it to its natural state. There are a variety of techniques for this, but I like what's called foursquare breathing because it's simple to do and remember:

1. Breathe in for a count of four.
2. Hold your breath for a count of four.
3. Exhale for a count of four.
4. Wait and do not breathe for a count of four.

Start out doing this for ten cycles. Work toward breathing more slowly and deeply during each cycle. Again, this is an exercise you can do every day, as it will take you only two to three minutes, which isn't really that much time. If you are hyperventilating, the last step will be challenging because you'll feel like you need to take another breath. Wait, however, and complete the cycle. Hyperventilation and its symptoms of disorientation, feeling antsy or jittery, rapid pulse, and tingling are all wrapped up in the symptoms of anxiety and a panic attack. Foursquare breathing can help you avert a full-blown panic attack by calming your breathing and slowing down your entire system.

Mini-vacation. There are reasons people travel to exotic, tropical locales on vacation. These places are pleasant to get away to. They're also, usually, far away, at least physically. One of the relaxation techniques I like involves taking a quick getaway without ever leaving. It's a mental getaway while your body stays put.

1. Find a quiet place.
2. Close your eyes and imagine a peaceful place where you feel comfortable.
3. Breathe deeply and slowly.
4. Imagine what this place looks like, feels like, smells like, sounds like.

If you have access to a portable CD player or iPod, download sounds that correspond to your mini-vacation locale. Wonderful relaxation selections include natural sounds of the beach, rain, wind blowing, birds, or soft, soothing music. If you are going to utilize a recording for this, keep it turned down low, just above hearing level. The goal is to relax, not blow out your eardrums. This is something that can be done for about ten minutes.

For those of you who are perfectionists and are now thinking how much you could actually get done in those ten minutes, don't dismiss this activity out of hand. Taking a short break can actually increase productivity. If ten minutes seems too long, take five. For those of you who tend to shut down and do nothing, couple this activity with a task you know you need to do but are putting off. Take your mini-vacation first and then tackle the other task (we'll talk more about this in chap. 12).

It's been my experience that anxious people are amazingly creative when contemplating disaster. Their imaginations run wild in the direction of catastrophe. This is an exercise that allows you to use your prodigious imagination in a positive way. As you identify your mini-vacation locale and return on a regular basis, allow your mind to continue to fill in calming details. Maybe at first you just hear the water, but later you're able to visualize how it moves, what color it is, how the sun reflects off it, how it feels as it gently laps against your skin. Your mind has been taken hostage so often by imagined terror; it's time to reclaim your imagination for your good.

Progressive muscle relaxation. Have you ever noticed how relaxed you can feel after you've done something physically strenuous? It's possible to relive a little of this feeling by engaging in progressive muscle relaxation. You can do this sitting up or lying down. The goal is to tighten specific muscle groups in your body, hold the tension, and then release it and move on to the next muscle group. You can start with your face and neck and work down your body, or you can start with your toes and feet and work up. Some people have a particular area of their body that holds their stress, and they will either start with that area or end with it. There aren't any rules to this exercise, so you can personalize it in ways that work best for you. Your aim is to tense, hold, and release your entire body and then spend a few minutes enjoying the residual relaxation.

Some people find it helpful to listen to a CD of instructions for progressive muscle relaxation. We have one at the Center, recorded by the facilitator of our stress and relaxation class. Again, if you're going to use one of these directed recordings, keep the volume as low as possible.

This relaxation exercise takes about twenty minutes, so you'll want to allow for enough time. As your body becomes more familiar and you become more comfortable with this relaxation technique, you'll find you can gain similar benefits in shorter amounts of time. Again, for you perfectionists, this isn't some sort of race to see how fast you can get it done. The goal is to allow your body to relax, which won't be helped if you spend the exercise anxiously watching the clock.

Walking unplugged. Have you ever considered how much of your day you are surrounded by noise? Think about all the regular noise of everyday life, from machinery running, cars, and traffic to people talking and phones ringing. Then there is the noise we bring upon ourselves. We have the television on, the radio on, and we're plugged into our iPods. Noise demands attention; noise produces physical and emotional stress. Stress unaddressed, even stress that runs under our radar, is draining and depleting. Stress needs to be dealt with, and when the goal is relaxation, one of the best ways to reduce stress is to engage in physical activity. There are a variety of ways you can physically deal with your stress, but one of the best things to do is simply take a walk.

Anxious people, however, often take their anxieties with them wherever they go, even on something simple like a walk. What should be a relaxing opportunity to enjoy the beauty around them becomes a tunnel-visioned race to outrun their inner fears, as their worries and cares pound out a constant drumbeat in the background of their thoughts. To cover up this drumbeat, anxious people will listen to music while walking or exercising. The louder the inner drumbeat, the higher they need to turn up the volume. This is not relaxing. It may be distracting momentarily, but it is not relaxing.

The next time you take a walk, I encourage you to unplug from your headsets and earbuds, from your noise. Instead, take silence with you as your walking companion. Become acquainted with your own thoughts and your own mind. Hold on to a positive attitude. If you find yourself thinking negative thoughts, counter with positive affirmations about yourself. This is an excellent time to put into practice what you learned in chapter 8 about turning up positive thoughts and turning down negative thoughts. When you're not barraged by other people's thoughts or sounds, you'll be better able to hear your own. The better you hear your own thoughts, the more you'll learn about yourself. The more you learn and know about yourself, the more relaxed you can be with simply being you.

Working out. As someone who's been a runner for years, I know the relaxing benefits of a good workout. This is one of the best ways for your body to burn off the stress from anxieties and achieve a state of relaxation. Walking is one way to do this, but there are many others, depending on your preferences. Some people play a team sport like basketball or softball. Others swim or bike. Some go to the gym. If you have not incorporated physical exercise into your daily life, I encourage you to consider it, after consultation with your primary care physician, of course.

Whatever you decide to do to enhance your ability to achieve relaxation, I cannot encourage you enough. Relaxation isn't some sort of reward given out only when you've "earned" it. Relaxation isn't a zombie state of inactivity. Relaxation is your mind intentionally assisting your body to reap the benefits of a calm and restful state.

Deep sleep. The ultimate altered state for relaxation, of course, is sleep. If you are anxious, sleep is difficult to achieve and difficult to maintain. You may have trouble falling asleep or find yourself waking up in the middle of the night, unable to fall back asleep. Some anxious people experience the opposite. They sleep a great deal, more than normal, but wake and are still exhausted. Being sleep-deprived creates stress, which ties right into an anxious state. Getting proper rest is one of the best ways to fight the effects of anxiety and stress.

Each of the relaxation methods we've discussed, when practiced regularly, can help you decrease your stress level. A decrease in your stress level can produce a corresponding increase in your ability to experience restful sleep. There are other techniques you can use to assist in falling and staying asleep.

- *Keep to a regular sleep schedule.* I try not to vary, by much, the time I go to bed and wake up each day of the week, including weekends. This establishes a pattern for my body. Establishing a pattern alleviates anxiety through repetition and familiarity.

- *Prepare your sleep environment.*

  keep it dark

  keep it quiet

  keep it a comfortable temperature

  sleep on a good quality, supportive mattress

  have good airflow in the room

When you are anxious, any difficulty with your sleep environment is magnified. Do yourself a favor and cut down on the distractions to sleep. Fewer distractions give your worries and fears fewer opportunities to gain a foothold in your sleep.

- *Do not use tobacco or alcohol from late afternoon on.* Some people use smoking as a way to cope with anxieties, but nicotine is a stimulant, which is the last thing an anxious person needs to introduce into their body. We've already gone over the negative effects of alcohol in chapter 4. The goal is not to use either of these to self-medicate your anxiety, but if you haven't stopped doing so, at least make sure to avoid using them from late afternoon on.

- *Keep your bedroom your bedroom.* Anxieties don't respect a lock on a door, so you'll need to intentionally banish them from the bedroom. One way to discourage your concerns and encourage your sleep is to be intentional about what you allow inside. Don't turn your bedroom into an auxiliary television room, computer room, or workstation. Your bedroom should be a place where you give your mind and body permission to rest, to turn off, and go into sleep mode.

- *If you have trouble sleeping, try warm milk.* This may be an old remedy, but warm milk does have properties that can help you sleep. You can also use a small cup of noncaffeinated hot tea. Drink four to six ounces rather than twelve to sixteen ounces, or you'll end up waking up during the night to use the bathroom!

- If you're having trouble sleeping, *turn the clock around so you can't see it*. Watching the changing time isn't going to enhance your ability to relax and fall asleep. Instead of fixating on the time, try taking a mini-vacation.

- Some people find it relaxing to *take a hot bath or shower just prior to going to bed*. Allowing your body to relax physically will assist your mind in triggering its shut-off switch. This works well in conjunction with progressive muscle relaxation.

- You can always *use one of the relaxation techniques* talked about in this chapter. Some you can do as you're lying in bed preparing for sleep, and others, such as exercising or walking, you can do during the day to facilitate sleep at night.

ANCHORING ACTIVITY

You've read several suggestions in this chapter to help you work on your ability to relax. It is an ability, one that can be learned and improved upon. But before you can learn to do something better, you first need to discover what you think about it in the first place. So I'd like you to think about the ways you relax now:

- What do you consider a relaxing thing to do?
- How often do you find yourself relaxing during the day?
- How often do you find yourself relaxing during the week?
- Do you wish you could relax more?
- Are you afraid of falling asleep? Does it seem like a loss of control?
- Are you envious of people who appear to be able to relax and not worry about it?

- Do you hold off relaxing until you feel you've "earned" it? If so, how do you earn your relaxation?
- What do you use to help you relax? Do you eat to relax? Drink to relax? Exercise to relax?
- How often during the day do you feel relaxed?
- How often during the day do you feel anxious or stressed?
- How often during the day do you spend time just quietly sitting or thinking?
- Which of the relaxation suggestions presented in this chapter are you going to start incorporating into your life?
- When you're comfortable with that strategy, which one will you try next?
- How committed are you to making the changes you need to make to enjoy a life filled with more times of relaxation?
- What are you willing to give up to make room for relaxation in your life?
- How committed are you to taking back control over your life, including your ability to relax, from your fears and concerns?

The last question is really the crux of the matter. You need to be committed to taking back your life. Otherwise, your anxieties will continue to dominate.

Before we leave this topic of relaxation, there is another way to find relaxation in this life. It is through a loving relationship with the Creator God and his Son, Jesus. Neither wants you to live a stressed-out, anxiety-ridden life. Eugene Peterson, in the *Message*, records Jesus's words in Luke 12:29–32 this way: "What I'm trying to do here is to get you to relax, not be so preoccupied with getting so you can respond to God's giving. People who don't know God and the way he works fuss over these things, but you know both God and how he works. Steep yourself in God-reality, God-initiative, God-provisions. You'll find all your everyday human concerns will be met. Don't be afraid of missing out. You're my dearest friends! The Father wants to give you the very kingdom itself."

If you want to relax, to find peace and contentment, spend time with God and meditate on the amazing person and gift of Jesus. For years, many of you have given countless hours to knowing every one of your anxieties, worries, cares, and fears inside and out. You're more intimately aware of their presence in your life than you are of God's. Think about Jesus's words and intentionally reject the illusion of anxiety and steep yourself in God-reality. God-reality is a place where he is sovereign, in control, and working to produce the greatest good in your life.

Like David, O God, allow me to say, "My soul finds rest in God alone; my salvation comes from him." Help me to find rest in you, to be able to turn from the cares of this life and relax in your presence, in your peace, in your provision. Calm my fears. Turn down the noise of my worries. In the quiet moments, let yours be the only voice I hear. Thank you, Jesus.

11

Relief through Exposure

Make Progress with Baby Steps

Bill could remember right when it started. It came out of the blue, really. He'd been driving home from a trip out of town, not really paying much attention to his surroundings, thinking about the sales call he'd been on and wondering if he'd been successful. Only marginally aware of his surroundings, he was startled by brake lights popping on up ahead. Just as he entered a tunnel, he had to stop suddenly. It was raining, with limited visibility, so the traffic snuck up on him pretty fast. He remembered being a little shocked but glad he'd been able to stop in time. Some sort of pileup ahead had backed things up.

Accident averted, Bill waited for his heart rate to go back down, but it didn't. For no apparent reason, he started to feel extremely uneasy. He felt uncomfortable in the tunnel. The light was dingy, and soot-covered fluorescents were spaced evenly over generic graffiti. It was an old tunnel with pale tile walls, and it wasn't very wide, just two lanes, which explained the backup. The longer he waited, the more the walls seemed to close in on him. His breathing picked up, and he started to sweat. He could feel his heart thumping in his chest.

Panicking, he started to think about what would happen if he had a heart attack. Was he that stressed out about the trip? Had there been other signs he'd missed? What were the signs of a stroke? He had meant to give up smoking but hadn't. What would it mean if it was a heart attack? What would he do? How would he get help? He tried to settle his breathing and put his head on the steering wheel, attempting to relax. He just needed to relax, that's all. But the more he identified the need, the farther away it seemed. He decided he needed to get out of that tunnel, but he was stuck. By the time traffic started moving again, Bill was shaky, sweating, and couldn't wait to get out.

That was the beginning—his introduction to the ambush of fear. He was so afraid of being attacked again that any condition resembling the tunnel experience was considered dangerous. It didn't have to be a tunnel; it could be a long overpass. Anywhere he was in shadows, he'd come under that sinking feeling again.

Where before driving had been something Bill did without thinking, now he paid close attention. If he had to go somewhere, he mapped it out carefully to make sure there were no tunnels. If he deemed a route safe, he drove that way all the time. The goal with driving wasn't just to get where he wanted to go but to get there without triggering an attack. Bill would do just about anything to avoid another attack. Traveling had become unsafe, which wasn't really a good thing for a salesman on the road.

Anxiety whittles away at your choices in life. Fear of one thing often expands to fear of two things, then three, in a ripple effect. Before long, you find yourself giving up a great deal of life to avoid even coming close to a source of fear. It's like the fear of falling off a ledge. When the fear hits, an inch from the edge screams absolute danger. You're still firmly standing on the ledge, but the proximity to the danger of the edge makes that inch an unacceptable risk. An inch away is now the new edge. An inch becomes a foot. A foot becomes a yard. But the fear just keeps expanding until you're farther and farther away from the actual edge.

Bill found himself spending more time planning his sales routes than actually working them. His income began to drop, increasing his anxiety. As his anxiety increased, his sense of safety diminished. Within two months of the tunnel incident, Bill had another panic attack, this time driving along the bottom level of a long bridge. He'd managed to pull over to the side before he lost control of the car, but it had been close. How was he supposed to continue his job with the specter of a panic attack waiting every time he stepped out the door and into his car? Fear expanded, and his world shrank. His world shrank, and so did his income. His income shrank, and fear expanded. This was an unacceptable spiral.

Bite-Sized Fear

Although Bill was afraid of driving, he was even more afraid of losing the quality of his life. He had a choice; he could allow his world to shrink or he could go out and face his fear head-on. Bill chose to do the latter. Together, we used a technique called progressive exposure, also known as systematic desensitization. I tend to think of it as baby steps. Instead of tackling the big, huge fear, you work at conquering your fear one small step at a time. It's a way of taking the monster of your fear and cutting it down to size, or put another way, it's taking that huge helping of fear and reducing it to bite-sized pieces. You incrementally and intentionally expose yourself to what you fear in small steps. Exposure doesn't sound like a good thing when dealing with fear, but it's the only way to tame the monster.

Several years ago, I worked with a woman who, like Bill, experienced a panic attack without warning. It occurred in an elevator in a Seattle high-rise. Traveling up to the eighteenth floor, stressed and worried about a business presentation, Anita remembered hearing a loud clunk. It was as if the weight of her worries and fears collapsed into that single sound, making the density of her fear unmanageable and dragging all logic and reason into an emotional black hole. By the time she reached her destination, she was convinced she was having a heart attack. After she hyperventilated to the point of passing out, the paramedics were called. Utterly humiliated and deeply frightened, Anita realized her presentation was ruined, but that wasn't all; so was her peace of mind. Terrified of being so out of control again, she lost her ability to ride in an elevator. Even using the stairs, Anita told me, became impossible. The higher up she climbed, the harder each step became until she buckled under the fear, unable to go farther.

On the surface, it appears easy to identify the source of Bill's and Anita's fear: for Bill, it was tunnels; for Anita, it was heights. However, it wasn't that simple. Both found their fear to be progressive, and both became terrified not only of the initial condition but also of the condition of fear itself. Bill and Anita became hypervigilant about how they were feeling at any given moment. Each reported feelings of being disconnected, of feeling like they were becoming unhinged from reality and pulled into a state of escalating panic. Bill's fear started in a tunnel but progressed to the act of driving itself. Anita's fear started in an elevator but progressed to the physical act of climbing.

The way to combat the progressive nature of fear is to combat it with another form of progression. The escalation of fear makes it seem impossibly big; to tackle it, you've got to cut it down to size. Then, starting small, you progressively work your way up the ladder of your fear, becoming if not comfortable at least tolerant of each progressive rung.

To climb up this ladder of fear, it's important to identify each rung. For Bill, the first rung of fear started each morning as he contemplated having to get in his car and drive somewhere new or unsafe. He tended to make excuses for staying home and working the phones or email instead of actually seeing customers. As he climbed higher and higher up his fear, he got to the point where he became stressed making new calls or talking to certain customers because of the fear of what he would be asked to do. Salesmen are trained to say yes to customers, and Bill was in constant conflict that his fear would require him to say no—no to someplace new, no to a face-to-face meeting, no to having to drive.

As we took apart Bill's fear and started to look at it in smaller chunks, it became evident that the fear wasn't a single, gargantuan one. Instead, Bill's fear was made up of smaller, debilitating fears that forged a paralyzing partnership in that tunnel. That day, the tunnel seemed small and threatening, but the tunnel was only a representation of how pressured and squished Bill already felt about himself and his life.

Bill hadn't been merrily driving down the road, whistling a happy tune, before the brake lights ahead caught his attention. Bill had been stressed and fearful even before he'd gotten into his car to drive home that day. In the back of his mind, he was worried, always worried, about his job, about his health, about where he found himself in life. At fifty-three, he literally and figuratively wasn't happy with where he was headed. He fretted about nearly everything. All of his life, he came to realize, he felt as if he was being dragged along by circumstance, never fully in charge, always reacting to whatever happened to him. He never felt like he could stop long enough to get his bearings and make decisions. He felt life made decisions for him, and he was forced to go along.

When I asked him how long he'd felt that way, he said as long as he could remember. His childhood had been chaotic. After his parents divorced when he was eight, he moved four times before graduating from high school. He kept hoping tomorrow was somehow going to turn out better than today, but it never seemed to happen. Instead, tomorrow kept handing him challenges he felt unable to deal with: a new school and new kids to try to make friends with; how to pay for college; what to do for a job when nothing really excited him; what to do with his life when college didn't work out; how to find a relationship and then how to get over one. At fifty-three, Bill felt he was running out of enough tomorrows for everything to turn out right.

That night in the tunnel, fear of failure, fear of pain, fear of lost time and lost opportunities, fear of loneliness, fear of living for less, and fear of death all came together. By identifying each rung of the fear ladder, Bill was able to begin to separate the individual components of this fear experience. For example, he realized that the fear he felt now upon waking was acute fear of failure. Before a day started, success was possible. However, once it started, Bill could feel the fear of failure rising. The fear he felt making cold calls was the fear of lost time and opportunities because it seemed so often his expectations never lived up to reality. The more boxed in he felt while driving mirrored how boxed in he felt about his life. The tunnel, finally, was actually the fear of death, so traumatic had been the physical shock of the panic attack, as his body turned against him, and for the first time he felt as if he was going to die. And he wasn't ready, not the way he felt about himself and his life.

Recognizing this deep-seated fear of death allowed Bill to clarify his dissatisfaction with life. He'd been making all sorts of excuses and just running faster and faster, trying to get away from this pervasive sense of dissatisfaction and regret. It caught up with him in the tunnel.

Step by step, Bill worked to advance up each rung of his fear ladder. This wasn't easy. He had to stay longer on some rungs than others, holding on and working through his fear in order to advance to the next level. Along the way, Bill utilized a variety of relaxation techniques and a good deal of therapy, or coaching. As soon as he was able to tolerate a certain level, he was ready to go on to the next. It was almost anticlimactic by the time he tackled returning to the actual tunnel. He found the tunnel had returned to being just a tunnel. Instead of thinking of it as a place where his life had almost ended, Bill started to think of it as a metaphor for when his life—a life of choices and control—started.

Staying Grounded

When fear takes over, you feel like you're being sucked into a ter-rifying maelstrom without any control or ability to stop. Your panic races ahead and leaves reason and logic crushed in its wake. Progressive exposure is a valuable way to slow down this racing and help you remain grounded. Panic leaves you feeling, like Anita experienced, unhinged. Taking on small, bite-sized pieces of your fear allows you to take on just enough to make progress and just enough to allow you to retain control. Bit by bit, you reclaim reality and push back the borders of the panic.

Working with Anita, we didn't use the analogy of a ladder, since her issue was heights. We used the analogy of baby steps. I told Anita it was like someone who has an accident and needs to relearn how to walk. Walking is something they knew how to do and something they can relearn, but they have to go through the process and get stronger every day. Anita liked this analogy because, as a teenager, she had broken her leg in a skiing accident and remembered the drive and determination needed to rehabilitate after her injury. She considered our work a sort of rehabilitation, a recovering of something she once had but lost.

We needed to work on rehabilitating her sense of perspective. Anita realized it wasn't about heights, that it was about so much more, but to recover she needed to relearn how to climb. Over the course of several months, we viewed pictures of office buildings and explored the reasons for her discomfort. We drove downtown and walked around the perimeter of several high-rise buildings.

We looked at them from blocks away, from across the street, from right alongside. We entered and exited their lobbies. We took short flights of stairs in shorter buildings. We took short flights of stairs in taller buildings. We stepped on and off elevators. We rode up one floor, got off, got back on, and rode down. Step by step by step.

Throughout this progressive exposure, Anita became very adept at her favorite relaxation techniques. She excelled at foursquare breathing and found that taking a mini-vacation before and after each challenge helped her refocus and relax. Even thinking about working through this process produced a degree of physical stress, so Anita decided she needed a way to work through it instead of stewing in it. She took up exercising again and joined several women in her neighborhood for regular early morning walks.

Bill's issue wasn't any more about a tunnel than Anita's was about an elevator. By working through each progressive step, Anita was challenged to deal with the underlying issues. As much as she knew it and was afraid to admit it, Anita was a controller. All of her life, as long as she felt in control, all was well with her world. She was capable, intelligent, energetic, and productive—as long as she felt in control. Anita realized how deeply suspicious and distrustful she was of anyone but herself. The clunk in the elevator was merely a reminder to Anita that, occasionally, she had to put her life in the hands of other people and that this was truly frightening. Riding the elevator became Anita's metaphor for learning to relax and trust others. Being an analytical person, she researched the actual dangers and risks involved with riding an elevator. This helped her put her fears in proper perspective. She still often takes the stairs, but only because she likes the exercise.

Taming the Monster

Big fears are a complex connection of smaller components. Fears generally have a time line—a when. They have a reason—a why.

165

They have a pattern—a what. They have an outlet, a venue for expression—a how. The type of counseling I use is called *cognitive-behavioral*. It's a method that addresses each of these components—the when, the why, the what, and the how. Cognitive-behavioral therapy incorporates the cognitive. Cognitive relates to your thinking and reasoning. Cognitive connects with your mind. By using your mind, you go back and discover the trigger point, the when, and you work toward uncovering the reasons, the whys. Cognitive is about what you think; behavioral is about what you do. Changing behavior requires a cognitive component, but once you understand and know the reasons and the background for behavior, you actually have to start doing something different. The behavioral component is about changing your behavior, taking what you do and doing something else, changing how you operate. When you understand when things started and why, you gain context. When you develop a strategy for changing your behavior, you change what you're doing and how you're doing it, allowing you to replace those old, negative patterns with new, healthier ones.

It can be tempting, in progressive exposure, to focus all your attention on the what and the how. Behavior is notoriously challenging to change. You must not shortchange the process. The what and the how give your monster shape, but the when and the why give your monster power. To truly tame your anxiety monster, you need to both resize it and deflate it so it doesn't blow itself back up again.

Taking the Steps

In this chapter, we looked at the examples of Bill and Anita, two composites of the many people I've worked with. Again, here are the steps I recommend for progressive exposure:

1. First, this has to be something you're willing to do, but it doesn't have to be done alone. Systematic desensitization works

very well in conjunction with regular counseling. Your therapist acts as a coach and encourager, helping you to prepare for, execute, and debrief after each step or rung of the process. You may find that you're able to make a certain level of progress on your own, only to be stymied at a particular point. Don't be afraid to call in reinforcements! If you're not able to work with a professional, sometimes you can call on a trusted friend to partner with you.

2. Before you start, practice the relaxation techniques and identify those that work best for you. Be comfortable with them in lower-stress situations, integrating them into your routine so they will be available to you when the stress stakes are higher.

3. If you experience several specific fears or concerns, start with the one you feel most able to tackle first, generally the one that causes you the fewest physical reactions. Then map out the course of your fear. If you want to, use the ladder analogy. Start at the bottom rung and chronicle each aspect until you reach the top— the thing or activity you fear, such as flying or heights or public speaking or talking on the phone or tight spaces. Where does the fear start and how does it progress? Remember to incorporate your relaxation techniques as you do this part, as even thinking about your fears is often enough to trigger them. Try as much as you can to analyze your fears as a third person. Give yourself permission to observe but not to react.

- To determine the first step, ask yourself, *Where does it start?* Try to trace your anxiety back to the beginning, to the point of first discomfort.

- On each rung of the ladder, ask yourself, *What happens?* Be specific about what is happening at this point. What are you doing? What are you feeling?

- Even after you arrive at each rung of your worry, don't stop there. Ask yourself, *Where does it lead?* What are you worried will happen? This is the part where honesty comes in.

You need to be honest with yourself about what you're really afraid of. Bill thought it was tunnels, but it was really dying while he felt a failure in life. Anita thought it was heights, but it was really losing control. Name your fear.

4. Keep working at it. You may find, once you start, that you need to reduce the size of your steps even further. The number of steps it takes to your goal isn't what's important; getting to your goal is. This is a journey to conquer your fear, but it is also very much a journey of self-discovery. It should be your goal through this process to learn about yourself and to love yourself. Love yourself enough to stick with it and not take defeat for an answer. You are bigger than your monster. Your life is more important than your fear.

5. Keep a journal. I know many of you won't actually do this, but I'm going to recommend it anyway. There is so much to be gained by taking on this challenge, and, realistically, unless you take the time to write something down, you're likely to forget it. This is worthwhile work, providing incredible personal insight. Value it by recording it. You never know who may need it in the future—you or someone else.

6. Give yourself the gift of time. It's the progress that matters, not the pace. Each of us is different, with different backgrounds and challenges. This isn't some sort of test to be aced; it's your life. It's worth the time and effort, so give it the effort and allow yourself the time.

7. No cheating. You will experience discomfort as you work through the process. In the past, you may have developed coping strategies that involve masking or numbing the discomfort. These are cheats and will negate your effort and work. Don't give in to them.

8. Don't be a hero. Again, you don't need to do this alone. The more debilitating the anxiety, the more you may need to work with a trained professional. Your Aunt Lucille or the neighbor down the street may be fine for tackling certain fears, but some

are entrenched and difficult to recover from without professional help. If you needed abdominal surgery, would you do it yourself? If you needed your transmission rebuilt, would you do it yourself? If you needed your house rewired, would you do it yourself? There is a time and a place for professionals. Don't feel bad—get the help you need.

ANCHORING ACTIVITY

Your activity for this chapter is simple: start. Take one of your fears—I'd encourage you to start small—and begin. One way to approach this is to think about what you do when you bake or cook. You decide what you're going to bake, you look over the recipe, and then you assemble the ingredients. With all the ingredients in hand, you follow the recipe and make the item. It's incremental and progressive. Do this exercise the same way. Decide what fear you're going to "bake." Look over the steps in this chapter, the "recipe" for success. Now assemble your ingredients. Do you need to find a friend or loved one to work through this with you? Do you need to locate a professional for help? What ingredients outside of yourself, what support structure, do you need for success? Once you've got your ingredients in hand, start the process. Go step by step until you arrive at the finished product—a reduction of your fear.

I can't do this for you. I can give you guidance and direction, but you've got to find this valuable enough in your life to undertake yourself. Be aware that even small fears have big voices. As soon as you identify the one you want to overcome, it's going to start yelling at the top of its little lungs why this won't work. This tiny terror is throwing a tantrum, and you're going to need to learn to acknowledge it and continue on anyway. Find the will to gather up the support structure you need to get the job done.

As you prepare to take these steps, I'd like to remind you that you truly are not alone. These steps you take in your journey to freedom over fear, to return to God-reality, are extremely important. Our loving Father is aware of the steps you are about to take and promises to be with you through each one of them. He understands about steps:

- Speaking of God, Job asks, "Does he not see my ways and count my every step?" (Job 31:4). Your steps are important to God, as you are important to him.
- Galatians 5:25 encourages you to keep in step with God's Spirit.
- In 1 Peter 2:21, we are reminded that Jesus left us an example so that we can follow in his steps. Recognize that your steps to recovery from fear are known by God, guided by the Spirit, and fully supported by Jesus.

Father, you desire for me to have an active faith, not a faith in word only. I choose today to step out in faith and address the fears that have held back my life and my faith. I need you to walk with me and to direct those steps. Comfort me when the fear strikes. Remind me that you are larger and more powerful than any of my fears. Help me to trust in the truth of your love instead of the presence of my fears.

12

Relief through Being Proactive

Take Care of Business

The email was short, just a reminder that the meeting started at seven o'clock and Judy would see her there. Sharon cringed, realizing she'd totally forgotten she'd agreed to attend that evening. She really hadn't wanted to go, but Judy had all but begged her, so she'd said yes, without any enthusiasm and, apparently, without any real desire to remember. Now her one peaceful evening at home was blown out of the water—so much for getting some laundry done and picking up that baby gift. Suddenly, Sharon found herself close to tears. It was all too much. She just couldn't keep up. Tonight was supposed to be her night to make some headway on her list. Now instead of headway, she felt herself slipping even more behind.

It wasn't just the meeting that was the problem. Sharon had agreed to help Judy clean up afterward. It wouldn't be much—just restacking the chairs and cleaning up the refreshments. It wouldn't take more than twenty minutes, but she had no idea how long the meeting would last. And it wasn't just tonight; it was all the nights—and days—stretching out in front of her, all the things she'd said yes to. Some of them she really wanted to do, or at least she had at the time. Now she just wanted to scream and not do *anything*. Most of the time at home now that's what she did—nothing. She just sat and watched television and tried to ignore all the things she was supposed to do.

She should have done the laundry over the weekend but hadn't. She should have picked up the baby gift when she was at the mall two days ago but hadn't. The baby shower was tomorrow, and she had to go, with a gift. She'd have to leave work during lunch. If she hurried, she could pick up something to eat, find a gift, and get back within an hour. Of course, she wouldn't have any time to wrap it, so that meant more money spent to get a gift box or bag.

No matter what she was able to pick up at the last minute, it wouldn't be what she wanted. When Sharon had first been invited to the shower, she'd envisioned finding the perfect little blanket or outfit and making a special card. She thought she'd have plenty of time, but, as usual, time had run out. Time was always running out, and Sharon felt she was always running, trying to catch up to her life.

Driving Force

Do you feel like you're always playing catch-up?

Does it feel like you've got too many things to do and not enough time, energy, or desire to get them all done?

Do you feel dragged along by life and all the things you think you must do?

Have you ever just wanted to run away and leave all of it behind, just to have a brief moment of peace?

Have you found yourself getting more and more irritated at the pace of your life and the fact that nothing and no one seems able to just leave you alone?

Are you perplexed by your inability to control your schedule or get anything done?

These are stress questions. In chapter 3, we talked about the effect stress has on your life. Over the years, I've been amazed at how many anxious, worried, fearful, and stressed-out people have answered yes to these questions. It's as if each successive task, duty, obligation, or requirement turns up a stress dial until they are permanently on the far side of overwhelmed. It's also amazing how many highly productive and competent people find themselves trapped in this category. These are the go-getter people, who are constantly going and going, constantly getting and getting, who find themselves drowning under the flood of their own agendas.

Then there are the others. They are not the go-getters; they are the stay-putters. These aren't people who wake up one day and feel overwhelmed by the frantic pace of their lives. Instead, the stay-putters have felt overwhelmed and inadequate all their lives. They don't identify with the loss of control of the go-getters because they never felt they had any control to begin with.

The answer for both groups—the go-getters and the stay-putters—is to grab the wheel of your life with both hands and decide you really are the driver after all. This can be scary at first. Sometimes you don't think you're the driving force in your life because other people have always told you what to do, where to go, how to think. You've been riding in the backseat of your life, allowing other people to decide the direction, and deep down it seems safer this way because you don't really trust yourself to make the right decisions. Sometimes you hide out in the backseat of your life because you've traded security for independence, safety for autonomy.

Sometimes you don't think you're in control of your life because you've got too many things pushing you from behind. You're in the driver's seat, but you're barraged by everything else you've invited into your car, into your life. They're yelling and struggling, demanding you take them here and there right now. All your agendas and tasks and agreed-to items are like a car full of screaming children crawling around in their seats. You're driving, but you definitely don't feel in control.

Even if you don't think you're in control of your life, you are. You are in control of the most important aspect: how you view yourself and your life. This is your starting point. This is where you reconnect with reality and start taking charge. Worries, fears, and anxieties are more than happy to drive your life. They'll take you to places you don't want to go, to experiences and feelings you don't want to have. Either you can stay huddled in the backseat, at the mercy of whatever grabs the wheel at any given moment, or you can stop long enough to accept responsibility for your life and decide to drive it yourself. You can continue to allow a car full of unruly obligations to make driving a nightmare, or you can stop long enough to get control of your chaos. Either way, you've got to take charge of your life to reduce the stress that's fueling your anxiety.

Claim Ownership

The first step to taking charge is claiming ownership of your life. Other people may have influenced it, circumstances may have impacted it, but it is your life. The life you live today is the product of your own making. You may not have chosen all the situations you find yourself facing, but you have chosen how to respond to each of them. You have decided your priorities by what you choose to do and what you don't. Every action you take in any given moment, in any given hour, in any given day, is a choice. You've been choosing how to react based on your anxieties. To reclaim your life, you need to learn to make different choices. Responding to life, instead of reacting to it, allows you to take charge.

174

Weed Out Your Worry

Worries are like weeds; they have a tendency to grow up overnight. One of worry's favorite, most-fertile soils is an over-busy life. An overcommitted, no-time-to-breathe daily pace produces a toxicity that poisons peace, calm, and contentment. On the other hand, worries thrive in this toxic environment. When you're so busy going from thing to thing, there's no time to stop, to evaluate, to determine your next course. There is no time for reflection. There is no time to take a breath and decide what to do next. When there's no time for you to decide, you've lost control.

This is what you started in chapter 9—this weeding out of the small stuff in your life. These small things seem little and inconsequential, just like weeds, but left unchecked they'll take over your life. So how's your weeding going? How did you do with the anchoring activity in that chapter? How are you doing cleaning house on those net negatives in your life? This weeding-out process is going to take time and discipline. You've got to keep at it.

I've heard several people I've worked with over the years bemoan their inability to say no. This is given as the reason why their lives are unmanageable. Sure, I'm interested in why they can't say no, but I'm also interested in why they keep saying yes. Each yes is a choice, and each choice reveals something about who they are as a person. Each yes highlights their priorities. When you purposely keep saying yes to the small stuff that complicates your life, it says something about your priorities. When you purposely keep saying yes to the small stuff that complicates your life, it says something about your anxieties.

I've also worked with people over the years whose vocabulary rarely included the word *yes*. Every yes constituted a risk, so they just kept up a steady stream of no. Worries can quickly become thick in your life; they choke out space for anything else to grow. By constantly saying no to life, these people were actually saying yes to their anxieties. This isolation suited their anxieties just fine.

Reclaim Your Priorities

What you say no to and what you say yes to define who you are and reveal your priorities. To take charge, you need to reclaim your own priorities. This presumes, of course, that you know what they are. You may have been living with your anxieties' priorities in charge for so long that you've forgotten your own. It's time to reclaim them. Once you've rediscovered what's important to you (we'll do this together during this chapter's anchoring activity), you can use these priorities as a filter to evaluate what you've said yes and no to. You can use them as a filter to decide if and where to make changes in what you're doing. The goal is to include those activities that enhance your life and priorities and find the courage to jettison those that don't.

Stay Organized

It's an undeniable truth that orderly things don't stay that way without effort. Banished worries and jettisoned activities have a tendency to creep back into your life. You'll need to be aware of this tendency and be on guard against it. The best way I know of is to develop habits that encourage you to stay organized.

When you know what your goals are for each day and what you need to achieve, you're able to organize your time. The challenge here for busy people is to include goals such as reflection, rest, communication, and play. The challenge for busy people is to expand their definition of achievement to include the value of these things in their lives. These activities act as brakes, as a means to help you slow down and regenerate from even the most hectic of days. The challenge for sedentary people is to include goals such as accomplishment, completion, progress, and attainment. These activities act as accelerators, with one success propelling you toward the next.

176

Stay Active

Staying organized gives you control over your life and thwarts one of the prime companions of worry: procrastination. Procrastination has the ability to transform a molehill into a mountain, as small things that perpetually get put off have a tendency to grow out of control. The bigger they grow, the harder they are to tackle and the easier they are to put off.

One of the people I worked with couldn't seem to take action, even action he knew was needed or beneficial. It was as if Jon became frozen when confronted with the need to act. Taking action was unsafe, so he continually found ways to avoid it. He became adept at rationalizing and could make elaborate excuses for putting off doing what he knew needed to be done. Each undone task created its own pressure and produced its own consequence. The more things left undone, the more chaos swirled in Jon's life.

By the time he came to work with me, his life was a cluttered mess of deferred duties, undone tasks, and unfulfilled responsibilities. Other people went around cleaning up his messes and resented Jon for it. His family had withdrawn from him because he was unreliable in all things except one: if he said he'd do something, he could be counted on not to. This wreaked havoc with all his relationships except one: his deep relationship with fear of failure.

Fear of failure stopped Jon from taking action. He was more than willing to let other people act for him because it felt safer and more comfortable that way. Over the years, however, he found fewer and fewer people willing to act on his behalf, and more and more vital decisions were left unmade. His adult children wanted nothing to do with him. His wife had become more like his mother, having lost all respect for him, relegating herself to a caretaking role in his life as their intimacy faded.

Together, we started a candid exploration of the consequences of his perpetual procrastination. We looked at Jon's pattern of selective procrastination. For example, he was extremely timely in securing things he wanted, such as an early morning tee time on a Saturday at a popular golf course or obtaining the latest electronic gadget before others. In all things diversionary, Jon was ahead of the curve.

We talked about his aversion to accomplishing tasks. We talked about how his fear of failure had morphed over the years into resentment and anger at having to do anything that made him uncomfortable or that he simply didn't want to do. As a consequence, Jon wasn't living his life; he was deferring and complicating it, with fewer people willing to share it.

Worries and anxieties are encyclopedic about why you should put off action. There is always a reason why, when you don't really want to in the first place. It takes discipline to forge ahead and clean up that mess or take care of that item or make that call or schedule that appointment or handle that problem. Worries and anxieties would much rather have you spend an hour worrying about it than five minutes doing it—and being done with it and realizing it wasn't nearly as bad as you thought it was going to be so maybe next time you won't worry about it as much. Worries and anxieties want a monopoly on your time; they'd much rather have you stay actively engaged in fear with them instead of actively engaged in living your life.

Live in the Present

Dealing with today's problems, challenges, issues, and tasks today keeps you grounded in today. When you're in a state of worry, you're reliving the problems of the past and dreading the future. What's happening right now gets lost in the comparison of what did happen or could have happened and what might happen. The context of today is lost. To take charge of your life, you need to fight against anxiety's tendency to pull today apart in opposite directions—past and future—until it completely loses its shape and context.

Worry is the ultimate recycler. Any anxiety, fear, or concern is reused and recycled endlessly. Worry says if it happened once, it will happen again. Worry says just because it didn't happen doesn't mean it couldn't have. Worry says just because it didn't happen doesn't mean it won't. Worry says there's no guarantee about tomorrow unless it's a guarantee of disaster. Worry wants to heap up all the actual and perceived disasters of yesterday and pile them on today, as well as any possible problem of tomorrow. This is simply too heavy a load for today to bear; it will crush beneath the weight. Hope gets crushed, joy gets crushed, optimism gets crushed, as does any sense of perspective.

To take charge of your life, you need to start keeping today in line with today. Assess what is happening now and act accordingly. Open your eyes to the lines that demark past and future as you decide what to do. Keep today strictly in its borders and don't allow fear to fudge the edges. This used to be called stopping to smell the roses. Living in the present allows you to see the roses in the first place because you're focused on what's right up ahead. It allows you to stop without being whisked away by the momentum of the past and the propellant of the future. It allows you to breathe in deeply, acknowledging the amazing fragrance of the day. When yesterday is seen through the lens of fear and negativity and tomorrow is viewed as a disaster just waiting to happen, how can anything that happens today be seen as positive? Living in the present gives each day a chance to be viewed as the gift it is.

Deal with the Real

It is so important, as you work toward taking charge of your life, that you begin to insist on dealing with reality instead of perception. Sharon spent her life saying yes to far too many things because she was terrified of what people would think of her if she said no. Approval was everything to Sharon, and she thought the only way to get it was to say yes to others. So when Judy asked her to go to that meeting, Sharon said yes because she was afraid Judy wouldn't like her if she said no.

That was Sharon's perception, but it wasn't the truth. In reality, Judy would have been disappointed if Sharon had said no, but she would have understood. In reality, Judy would have been more than disappointed if she knew Sharon had said yes out of obligation and not out of a real desire to spend time with her. In reality, Judy's friendship with Sharon wasn't based on Sharon always saying yes. In reality, Judy was a better friend than that.

As I've counseled people, I've been amazed at how deceptive people can be to one another. But the person you and I are best at deceiving, above anyone else, is ourselves. To take charge of your life, you need to know what life is really about. You need to live your life in reality, looking for and acknowledging what is real and truthful, even if it hurts or is uncomfortable or triggers an anxiety. We have only one life to live here on earth; it makes no sense to squander so much of that life living in a state of denial about the truth that's going on around us and inside us.

If you refuse to acknowledge the dawning of the sun, you'll live your life thinking it's always night.

If you refuse to treat a broken leg, you'll live your life in pain and hobbled without understanding why.

If you refuse to factor in winter, you'll live your life wondering why you are so cold.

If you refuse to see a way to change, you won't.

Today and every day, in each situation you find yourself in, you have a choice. You can choose to look for the truth of the situation, or you can choose to settle for your perceptions. By settling for your perceptions, you refuse to consider other points of view or other possibilities. The stronger your fear, worry, or anxiety in any given situation, the sharper that perception. It can be so sharp that it rivals reality, but it's not. Start to look at life with more than the eyes of your fear and you'll be amazed at the view.

Figure It Out

As you get more adept at ferreting out the truth, the reality of what happens in your life, you'll be in a much better position to figure out what to do about it. It's difficult to come up with real answers to false situations.

Taking charge of your life means sometimes needing to come up with solutions to problems, problems you cause and problems you encounter as a normal part of living. Worry will attempt to complicate this process, because worry considers problems unwanted intruders instead of a normal part of life. Imagine a problem rings your doorbell. Worry flies around the room, ducking behind couches and hiding in closets. It jumps and screams and shakes its hands in terror, causing all kinds of action except the one that's needed. Someone's got to open the door. Worry doesn't want to do it. And even if it does, it's apt to slam the door and leave whatever problem you've got waiting outside. In my experience, waiting problems don't get better; they get worse. Someone's got to open the door. And that someone has to be you.

Once you open the door to your problem, you need to figure out how to fix it. By looking at the problem objectively, through the eyes of truth, you'll be farther ahead in figuring out what to do. The vision that allows you to see it truthfully will help you envision the way to fix it. This is possibility thinking; this is acknowledging and incorporating options; this is you taking proactive charge of your life and your problem.

Please be aware that once you open the door and acknowledge your problem, worries will come out of the woodwork, crawling over your resolve and obscuring your view of the solution. You'll need to be firm and insist on figuring this out on your own, with no "help" from your worries. Turn down their volume and turn up yours. Ask for advice from people you trust. Do your own research. It's your problem, and no one else can fix it for you. Don't procrastinate; figure it out. Taking charge of your life necessarily involves taking charge of your problem. When you take charge of your problem, you grant yourself the opportunity to redeem it for positives such as patience, maturity, understanding, insight, and growth.

Take Action

Figuring out how to deal with your problem has a couple of important components, so don't forget one of the most vital: when. It's not enough to decide what to do; you must decide when to do it. Again, don't procrastinate. Your ability to stop a problem in its tracks often has a particular time frame. Taking charge of your life means not only understanding what to do but actually doing it. Knowledge is a powerful thing, but it comes to completion in execution and application. Wisdom has been called the application of knowledge. Be wise and apply it.

Again, you'll need to apply the solution to your problem over the strenuous objection of your worries. When Jon began to make positive changes in his life, including disciplining himself to take action, his fear of failure became more strident at first. So he started small. He took it upon himself to retrieve the mail every day. This was something he'd always avoided because he was afraid of what he'd find lying in wait. At first, he said it felt like he was preparing himself for battle, just walking out to the curb and opening the mailbox. He practiced calming breathing and kept up a steady stream of internal encouragement to counter his fears.

As soon as he could tolerate retrieving and bringing in the mail, he started working with his wife to go through it. Eventually, he was able to assist her with paying the bills—something he hadn't done in years—and tracking the household budget. Step by step, he worked up the ladder of his fear one rung at a time. Before, Jon had always espoused grandiose plans of how to solve things and gave pointed direction to others on what to do. Now he waded into the waters of action himself. It's been good for his relationships.

Adjust as You Go

There is a trap waiting for those taking charge of their lives; it is the trap of rigidity. Worries are the cousins of rigidity; they are intimately related. If you are fearful of dying from a spider bite, all spiders are suspect, even though few are actually poisonous and even fewer have the ability to cause death. If you are afraid of flying, any commercial flight is life-threatening, even though it's safer than driving to the airport. If you're afraid of dogs, any canine you encounter is a danger, even if it's a twelve-year-old beagle whose only goal in life is to eat and be petted. If you're worried about food poisoning, you never eat any leftover, even if that's all you have in your fridge. Worries are rigid thinkers. They are excellent at constructing barriers in straight lines without exceptions.

You'll want to be aware of this relationship between worry and rigidity and seek to find ways around it. You work your way around rigidity by becoming more flexible. Flexibility in life means you adjust as you go. It's not dissimilar to the flexibility needed for a building project. Smart builders have something called a contingency fund. It's a percentage of the total construction budget set aside for when the unexpected happens. The best-planned projects factor in the unexpected—they expect the unexpected and adjust.

Life requires flexibility, an ability to bend. Rigid things that bend usually break. Flexible things can bend without breaking. Be flexible; factor in the unexpected *and be realistic*. If you insist on factoring in every contingency, even improbable ones, you're back to rigidity. Learn to adjust as you go, taking in the truth of the situation.

Stick with It

You need perseverance to move from baby steps to a mature stride. To take charge of your life and keep charge, you need to stick with it. These steps you're taking aren't simply a one-time application. You will need to apply them for the rest of your life. As daunting as that sounds, the more you work with them, the more familiar and comfortable they'll become. But this isn't a state achieved overnight; you need to stay the course.

ANCHORING ACTIVITY

You've allowed your worries and fears to have control over you; this is familiar ground, and they'll want to return to it. They won't like being kicked out and powered down. They will act up. When you've got the chaos of worries running and ducking for cover, when you've got them crawling over the control of your life, it can be difficult to remember what the focus is. Focusing can help you cut through the chaos and remember what's important, why you need to stay firmly in charge of your life.

To help you clarify your focus, I'd like you to think about your priorities—what they are now and what you'd like them to be. Again, be honest with yourself; live in reality. This is you, now, with all your anxieties. You need to understand what your current priorities are and how they are shaped by your anxieties. Once you've listed those priorities, I'd like you to uncover the fear or fears behind them.

If Sharon did this exercise, she would have listed her priorities as:

1. pleasing others
2. avoiding conflict
3. avoiding rejection
4. being loved

To Sharon, these were completely intermeshed. Pleasing others meant avoiding any sort of conflict that might lead to rejection and loss of relationship. At the core of these priorities was Sharon's fear: she feared she was an unlovable person. Sharon feared she was not worthy of being loved.

If Jon did this exercise, he would have listed his priorities as:

1. avoiding responsibility
2. deferring taking action
3. having others assume risk
4. having others fail

For Jon, his top priority was to avoid any sort of responsibility. To do that, he put off taking action and constantly looked to others to act for him, desiring others to be blamed for failure. At the core of these priorities was Jon's fear: fear of having the mask removed and being revealed as the failure he felt himself to be. Jon was a big talker to avoid being even a small doer.

Both Sharon and Jon ordered their lives around these priorities—these fear priorities—until their lives became unmanageable and they were willing to make a change. Are you ready to do the same?

What are your priorities, and what is the fear or fears at their core? It's okay to be afraid to look at yourself this deeply. It can be very uncomfortable, but do it anyway. If it helps, find a comfortable chair or pleasant surroundings. Take your time and take breaks if it becomes especially uncomfortable. Practice your calming skills and then continue. If you need additional support, work through this activity with someone you trust who loves you and supports you enough to help you do something worthwhile that's also difficult.

Take the time to do this exercise and tell yourself the truth. Open the door.

As I look at my life, these are my priorities:

1.

2.

3.

I've put down room for three. Examine yourself and try to come up with at least that many. If you uncover more, put them down.

Now, looking at these priorities in your life, what does this say about your underlying fear or fears? What fears are fueling your priorities?

1.

Try to identify at least one. Put down what first comes into your mind as you think of this, but don't stop there. Take a deep breath, relax for a moment, then continue. Examine this fear. Does it have any cousins? Are there others you can identify?

Now it's time to shift focus to you instead of your fear priorities. I want you to determine your goals in life. What do you want to do? What would you like to accomplish? What is important to you? If you have trouble thinking of these, think about what you feel your life is missing because of your fears. These could be your wishes, hopes, dreams, and desires struggling to come out from under the weight of your anxieties.

1.

2.

3.

4.

I provided space for four, but put down as many as you can identify. This is the content of your life freed from your fears. This is what you need to focus on when detaching becomes difficult and uncomfortable. This is the reminder of why the effort is so important.

It's time for your life to reflect you instead of your anxieties.

In Scripture, there is a metaphor of each one of us being like a house of God, a building for his habitation. In this chapter, we've been talking about doing some remodeling, some renovation to that house. We've been talking about removing some negative aspects of that house so that other positive aspects have room. I encourage you to remember that this remodel, this renovation, can be done with God's support. As you think about what you need to do and how you'll find the supplies and the strength to do it, consider this passage from 1 Chronicles, where King David is encouraging his son Solomon in his own remodeling project:

> Take charge! Take heart! Don't be anxious or get discouraged. GOD, my God, is with you in this; he won't walk off and leave you in the lurch. He's at your side until every last detail is completed for conducting the worship of GOD. You have all the priests and Levites standing ready to pitch in, and skillful craftsmen and artisans of every kind ready to go to work. Both leaders and people are ready. Just say the word. (28:20–21 Message)

Don't put this off. Just say the word. Decide to act and do it. God is with you in this. As he provided for Solomon, he will provide for you.

> *God, you are a God of action. You spoke everything into being. You hold everything together. I need you to hold me together, Father, as I begin to act for my own good. I have crafted my actions to support my fears. I choose today to craft my actions to support my trust in you. Today, help me to banish my fears and worship you as my God.*

13

Relief through Taking Charge
of Your Health

Learn to Make Good Choices

———◁◀▩◈▶▷———

Promptly at 9:30, Rita heard her co-worker start making the rounds in the office for the morning coffee run. She knew they wouldn't even ask her if she wanted any. It had taken about two weeks for the three who alternated the run to realize she really meant it when she said she didn't need anything. Rita used to be one of them, making the morning run herself, not so long ago. She said no now, but part of her still wanted to say yes—yes to that delicious jolt of hot delight, rich with flavor and caffeine, melting away her worries and fueling the rest of her morning. Rita wasn't afraid anymore to admit she was hooked, and she couldn't go back, at least not now. This time she was committed to making different choices, even if it meant putting up with the aroma that filled the office by ten o'clock each weekday.

There were so many changes to be made, changes Rita had put off for years until things had finally caught up with her. She'd started drinking coffee her junior year in high school as a way to keep her weight down and her energy up. Juggling classes and an after-school job, she never got enough sleep back then, except on the weekends, when she routinely slept past noon. Back then she paid attention only to how much she ate, not what. She went without eating whenever necessary, as defined by the way her jeans fit or whether she was dating anyone.

Rita had always been an anxious person, funneling her franticness into school and work and, occasionally, a relationship. Back then she hadn't paid too much attention to her edginess; it was just the way she was. She had accepted that she lived life at a fast clip, jumping from thing to thing, day to day, trying to keep up. Rita had been able to string herself along this way through a year and a half of community college, three part-time jobs, one full-time job, and two serious relationships. She kept thinking she'd calm down once her life slowed down, but it never seemed to.

The full-time job in her late twenties meant she finally had medical insurance and could get a routine physical, something she hadn't done since leaving home. Rita could still remember her feeling of shock when the doctor talked about putting her on high blood pressure medication. She remembered thinking, *Wait, isn't that for older people?* When had she become defined as older? She'd vehemently refused the medication and said she'd take steps to get her blood pressure down. Of course, the only real step she took was to avoid going back to the doctor. She'd started taking her blood pressure at the kiosk in the grocery store but gave that up too when the numbers flashing on the display never seemed to cooperate. She firmly decided to go with the age-old strategy of ignorance is bliss.

That changed after the panic attack. Three hours in the emergency room was a wake-up call. After all the testing to figure out what was wrong, Rita found out her physical condition hadn't improved in the past five years; it had deteriorated. Her weight was

189

up, her blood pressure was up, and her anxiety was definitely up. She felt emotionally and physically taut—increasingly stretched by the stresses in her life without a way to stop the pull. But it had to stop, she decided; she couldn't go on living this way anymore. Rita wanted to be free from the stress, from the worry; she wanted to be free from the feeling that peace was always an arm's length away. Rita was ready to lose the stress; it was the other things she needed to lose in the process that proved more difficult to give up.

Two weeks ago she'd given up coffee. She was determined to make better choices for herself and her health. She just needed to focus on what she was gaining instead of on what she was losing. As the rich smell began to permeate the air around her, Rita took a deep drink of her water and kept telling herself it was for the best.

There are some cars that have a high idle. Even if they're stopped at a light, the engine revs too high. When that happens, you have to push on the brakes hard so you don't lurch into the car ahead of you. Your gas mileage plummets because of the wasted energy. You wear out your engine; you wear out your brakes; you use too much fuel. A life full of anxiety is like a life on high idle. It's not good for you.

You live your anxiety life in your mind, but it is channeled through your body. Your body bears the consequences of the constant anxiety-driven, hyped-up state of fight or flight. Your worries and fears never give your body a chance to relax, to recharge, to renew. It's always revved up, straining to peel out in panic. It's time to enlist your body in managing and reducing your anxiety and stress level. It's time to treat your body differently and make positive choices that reduce anxiety.

Fixing Your Fuel

It really does matter what fuel you put in your body, just like it does with your car. If you use cheap, low-grade fuel in your car, you'll get uneven performance, engine stutters, backfire belches, and frequent stalls. There may be reasons for buying and using this type of gas—price, convenience, availability—but it's not really a bargain because of the short-term loss of performance and the long-term damage done to your car. If you use a more expensive, higher-grade fuel, made with components to handle the rigors of driving, your car simply runs better and lasts longer. Add in the recommended scheduled maintenance of tire rotations, oil changes, brake inspections, system flushes, and preventive replacements, and it becomes expensive and time-consuming to properly take care of your car. It takes more time and money, but, ultimately, you get more in performance, reliability, and longevity. As difficult as that concept is to grasp about cars, it's equally difficult to grasp about your body.

It is amazingly easy and convenient to feed yourself all the wrong things. You can cheaply fill yourself up with highly processed, fatty foods full of refined sugar. It is possible to go days, weeks, months, or longer without eating a green, leafy vegetable or an omega-rich piece of fish. You can sustain yourself with a steady diet of fast-food combos and convenience store options. The question, of course, is for how long and at what price.

At the Center, we treat the whole person, which means the emotional, relational, physical, and spiritual components of each individual. Over the years, we've learned how important the physical component is to treating issues like anxiety. When and what a person consumes through food or drink are extremely important. That is why we have naturopathic physicians and a registered dietitian on staff to help people take control of their physical well-being. We start with a few basics that are commonly overlooked or ignored. You already know what I'm going to say, but I'm going to say it anyway.

Eat a healthy diet. A healthy diet is one full of a wide variety of fresh fruits and vegetables. It includes whole-grain products, not highly processed ones. Lean meats, fish, and protein are also included, as well as low-fat dairy products for those who are able to digest them. These food choices should make up the majority of your daily calories, with the remainder being used for making sure you take in good fats from things such as fish and fish oil.

You know this; you've heard it and read it and ignored it over and over again. For the majority of you, this isn't news; you just haven't wanted to give up your comfort foods and ways of eating. You believe there is a benefit to be gained from continuing to eat and drink the way you do. It's time to jettison that belief, because it's false. When you live an anxious life, it puts stress on your body. Stress leaches nutrients and depletes you physically. A healthy, balanced diet deposits back in what life and stress take out.

Take a broad-based nutritional supplement, including vitamins, minerals, and amino acids. I live a fairly busy, complex life myself, and I am grateful for the benefits I gain from nutritional supplements. I don't know what I'd do if I needed to figure out all the different food combinations necessary to make sure I got enough selenium, magnesium, and zinc, to say nothing of the various vitamins with all their letters and numbers.

All these components—vitamins, minerals, and amino acids— are used for constant body building and renovation. They work independently of one another, but they also work in conjunction with one another. Some body processes will stop while waiting for the right component. When you eat a healthy, balanced diet and supplement properly, you're giving your body what it needs to function, including regulating your moods and refreshing and repairing itself. When you fail to provide your body with what it needs, you increase the physical stress on your body. It's like trying to run up a hill with emphysema. Running up a hill is hard enough without diminished lung capacity. When you starve your body of the nutrients it needs, while at the same time demanding it remain in a heightened state of anxiety, you're placing it in a difficult physical state with diminished capacity. Just like a car will break down, so will you.

Cut out caffeine. I know, I know, this one will be difficult for many of you. You practically live on caffeine, and the thought of doing without it makes you even more nervous. Anxiety revs up your body; so does caffeine. You need to eliminate caffeine in order to slow down your nervous system. Caffeine consumption doesn't calm you down; it hypes you up. It increases heart rate and blood pressure, both of which are already affected by your stress and anxiety. Replace the caffeine with water or noncaffeinated herbal teas if you need something hot.

Refrain from refined sugar. Sugar is a potent, mood-altering substance. It isn't always portrayed as such because of its common-ness, but ask any mother overseeing a group of six-year-olds after birthday cake and ice cream. Refined sugar can make you, quite literally, climb the walls. Sugar is a good-news, bad-news character. The good news is it's an energizer; the bad news is what goes up must come down. Sugar directly affects your blood glucose (sugar) levels. Blood glucose levels that spike precipitously also plunge the same way. When they plunge after an artificial high, it produces physical effects that mimic anxiety, such as shaking, sweating, and elevated levels of adrenaline and cortisol. This effect of climbing and falling blood glucose levels can precipitate the conditions of a panic attack. When you're in an anxious state, the last thing you need is a stimulant such as refined sugar. You need to eliminate it as a way to restore balance and calm to your nervous system.

Balance your blood glucose levels. By avoiding the ups and downs of blood glucose levels, you help stabilize your mood, decrease your physical symptoms of anxiety, and improve your overall energy. When people come to work with us at the Center, this is a vital area of education and support. We have seen it have a profound, positive effect. Our medical staff members educate people on incorporating both protein and complex carbohydrates into each meal and snack, increasing fiber and fat to help slow the release of glucose into the bloodstream. This slow release allows for the natural ebb and flow of blood glucose levels without the precipitous spikes or plummeting crashes. Our medical staff members help people understand how nutrition works—what to eat, how to eat, and when to eat to formulate a daily strategy for balance.

Maintain a healthy weight. I've spent the last twenty-five years of my professional career working with people with eating disorders. Notice I didn't title this paragraph "be thin." Instead, I said maintain a healthy weight. For some of you, a healthy weight means more than you are right now. For more of you, it means carrying less weight than you do right now. Being either too thin or too heavy stresses your body. It puts pressure on your heart, lungs, and nervous system and can contribute to feelings of anxiety, fear, concern, and panic.

Take out the artificial. As much as possible, eat whole foods and avoid highly processed, packaged ones. With a salad, you can see the lettuce, tomatoes, green peppers, and red onions. With a fresh chicken breast, what you see is what you get. With a handful of raspberries, you don't have to worry about artificial flavors, colors, or preservatives. These artificial additives cause many people problems. You can develop sensitivities and allergies to them, which in turn cause your body physical stress. As much as possible when you're looking over a list of ingredients, if you can't pronounce it, can barely read it, or it has over fifteen letters in it, maybe it's best to avoid it.

Be moderate. Remember, life requires flexibility. Having a piece of birthday cake or the occasional M&M is not going to drag you under nutritionally. Don't allow the rigidity of anxiety to find a new home in your refrigerator and kitchen cabinet. Be wise; be healthy; be moderate; be consistent. Remember the goal of healthy eating: to give your body the fuel it needs to function. This includes having the energy you need when you need it and being able to rest and relax.

Check out the pyramid. I recommend you work with a health-care professional to evaluate your eating and drinking habits and make positive changes to assist in reducing the physical symptoms of anxiety. I realize, however, that some people cannot afford an extended period of treatment.

Everyone may not have access to a registered dietitian or a naturopathic physician, but most people have access to the internet. There is a free government resource through the Department of Agriculture called the food pyramid, and it's found at mypyramid .gov. If you don't have access to the internet at home, you can go to any public library and ask for assistance getting to this site and printing the material. Or you can call the toll-free number on the website to order materials if you are unable to print them out yourself. The nutritional information provided is excellent, and you can obtain a personalized plan for your gender, age, and activity level that will explain what types and how much of foods to choose and how many calories you need each day to maintain a healthy weight. The site also contains extensive resource material on different types of food presented in an easy-to-understand format.

Work with a health-care professional. For those of you who are able, I encourage you to partner with a health-care professional in addressing your anxiety by improving your overall health. As I said before, we utilize naturopathic physicians and a registered dietitian at the Center. We also have a consulting medical doctor and psychiatrist. Our preference, whenever possible, is to incorporate natural, non-pharmaceutical solutions, but we recognize the value for some people of prescription medication, in the smallest effective dose possible for the shortest necessary time. We have come to this philosophy after a quarter century working with people suffering from anxiety issues, including our work in the realm of substance abuse and chemical dependency. Pharmaceutical medications have a valuable but limited role in the treatment of anxiety disorders. This is also a philosophy supported by the National Institutes of Mental

Health: "Medication will not cure anxiety disorders, but it can keep them under control while the person receives psychotherapy."[1]

It is vitally important for your health-care professional to be aware of all medications you're taking, including nutritional supplements, because the more complex the medications and supplements, the greater the potential for harmful interactions. For those of you whose source of anxiety is centered around your physical health, this is even more critical. You need to be able to assess the reality of your anxiety based on fact, not speculation or something you read in the checkout line at the grocery store. Some nutritional supplements and natural alternatives are very effective, but many are not. Some can be taken in combination with medications, and others cannot. You need to work with a professional who knows and understands both nutrition and medications and can provide you with accurate, reliable, and realistic information. The more that professional knows you, the better he or she will be able to assist you in making medical decisions for yourself.

Add exercise. Yes, I said it—exercise. For many of you, this word is not in your personal lexicon. It conjures up nightmares of grade-school gym class, stinky sweat, physical discomfort, and huffing and puffing. However, you're an adult now, and it's time to get over your middle-school distaste. As an adult, it's important for you to engage your body each day in some sort of physical activity. You don't need to train for a marathon, but you do need to find a way to use your body each day. It could be walking, gardening, taking the stairs instead of the elevator, or parking several blocks away instead of next to the door. If you don't like jogging, try water aerobics or a dance class or taking your kids to the park. Try taking a hike or engaging in a physical activity you haven't done in a while. We were not designed to be sedentary creatures, at least not optimally and not for long. If the word *exercise* still conjures up too many negative images, try the word *activity*. Consider yourself an active person consistently growing in activity. Stress and anxiety produce adrenaline that races around the interior of your body frantically trying to find a way out. Exercise provides one; it is an excellent way to reduce stress.

Your body is not just along for the ride where anxiety is concerned. It is intimately involved in how you feel and the effect your anxiety has on your life. You need to accept your body as an integral part of you, something you need to consciously and conscientiously treat properly and take care of. Your physical health is not incidental to your emotional health; they are interconnected. As you seek to take charge of your life, you need to include your physical health as well.

ANCHORING ACTIVITY

It's time to examine what you're eating and drinking. For you to get a balanced picture of your habits, I want you to do this for an entire month. What I've found is that people tend to be "good" when tracking for the first week or so but then revert back to reality. You can't change what you're doing if you're not dealing with reality. So go for thirty days. Guidelines for doing this include the following:

- Use a separate piece of paper for each day. Keep it with you during the day so you don't forget to write something down.

- Track what you eat every day, both weekdays and weekends. Many people have different rules for weekends, and I want you to have the full picture. You need to see the pattern of your eating across a broad span of time.

- Continue to eat the way you always do. You may be tempted to modify your eating habits because you're keeping track, but that will defeat the purpose. You need to be aware of what you're doing, not what you wish you were doing.

- Write down everything you eat and drink. That means everything that goes in your mouth. Everything counts, including water. You need to know how much you're eating and drinking and what. Track amounts. Whenever possible, write down the caloric values for each.

For tracking your food, I'd like you to use the categories of the food pyramid: grains, vegetables, fruits, milk, meat and beans, oils, and discretionary calories. For tracking your fluids, I'd like you to use four categories: water, caffeinated, alcohol, and other.

If you're being especially brave, write down what you're doing each day in the way of exercise or moving your body. If you're able, purchase a small pedometer and wear it. This will allow you to see how much you're really moving your body each day. A healthy body and a balanced system contribute to your overall health and ability to stabilize and maintain your moods. You feel better and sleep better.

Do you have a physician? If so, call now and make an appointment, setting the date to correspond with the end of your tracking so you can bring in the results. If you don't have a primary care physician, consider finding one and going in for a physical. Bring along your tracking. If you persist in doing this without a physician, be honest about what you're doing and the changes you know you need to make. At the very least, utilize the mypyramid.gov resources as you work toward improved health.

There is an absolute connection between mind and body. They affect each other, for good or for ill. Proverbs 15:30 says, "A cheerful look brings joy to the heart, and good news gives health to the bones." What you feel emotionally affects how you feel physically. As you seek to live a more positive life, looking for the good, don't neglect the health of your bones.

Father, I thank you for the body you have given me. I confess I do not take care of it the way I should. I need help and strength to care for it, to nurture it as you desire. Help me to understand the changes I need to make and the courage to do them. Give me perseverance and patience as I take the steps I need to restore health to my body. Protect me from my own excuses, fears, procrastinations, and refusals to do what I know I need to do. Empower me to act for my own good.

14

Relief through Resetting the Stage

Write Your Own Script

When Claire got home from work, she picked up the phone to check her messages. Over the past several months, she'd been working on reducing the anxiety this simple act produced. Claire was fearful of the phone. She didn't like to call and talk to people, and she especially didn't like picking up her messages. She'd been working through why that was and, as part of the process, had given herself the task of checking the phone each day for messages instead of putting it off for days like she used to.

Relax, she told herself as she picked up the phone and hit the code for messages. *They're just messages. They can't hurt you.* Claire knew her fear of the phone was really a fear of other people's expectations. Usually, when people left a message, it was either to provide information or to make some sort of request. The information she could deal with; she was working on dealing with the requests. *You don't have to say yes to everything*, she reminded herself. For Claire, requests represented a conflict between saying yes and remaining under the radar, going with the flow of others' expectations, and saying no, making herself much more visible and vulnerable.

Good, only three messages, she thought. *You can handle three.*

The first was the vet with a reminder she had an appointment in the morning for her cat. Yes, she knew about that one. That was easy; it was information. The second was from a survey calling for the third time that week. This she happily deleted. She could easily say no to this one because the request was from a far-removed, unknown party. The third was from her mother, asking her to call. It was short without any detail.

Why is Mom calling? Claire thought to herself, feeling her anxiety beginning to rise. *Don't panic*, she said to herself. *You don't know why she called. It doesn't have to be something negative just because you don't know.* Working to keep her breathing calm and steady, she punched in her mother's number. *There doesn't have to be a problem. Mom would have left more to the message if there was.* Using the timing of the rings to help with her breathing, Claire got the answering machine after the sixth ring. Briefly, she acknowledged getting the call and let her mom know she'd be home the rest of that evening.

She could just be out running an errand, she reminded herself as she felt the familiar knot trying to form in her stomach. Claire put down the phone and started preparing dinner. It wasn't long before she realized she wasn't really thinking about dinner; instead, she was still worrying about the phone call. *Go ahead and call Julie. If there's something really wrong, she'll know.*

Her sister answered quickly; she was busy putting her own dinner together. Claire told her about the message and asked if she knew the reason for the call. Julie told her she figured it was about getting Jessie's new address. Mom was fine. When Julie had talked to her yesterday, Mom said she'd misplaced the notice Jessie had sent out. Julie had admitted she couldn't remember where she'd put hers either and figured Claire would have it. She did. She gave it to Julie and then waited for her mom to call.

Okay, she concluded after she hung up with Julie. *That was okay.* Before, she would have put off calling for several days, absolutely terrified of the reason for the call, imagining multiple disastrous scenarios. She would have been embarrassed to admit her fears to Julie and wouldn't have called her either. And then when she had spoken to her mother, she would have been furious at her for causing a scare over such a little thing. This time they could have a nice, normal conversation without the tension. *Yeah*, Claire thought to herself, *without the tension.*

Claire made a conscious decision to write her own script regarding the situation with her mother. She could have quickly fast-forwarded into disaster, propelling herself into full-blown panic about the call, but she didn't. She stopped, evaluated what she knew, and composed the most probable scenario. When that did not alleviate her worry completely, she sought out additional information by calling her sister, filling in the blanks with knowledge instead of wild speculation.

Anxieties are all about wild speculation. The script they write never has a happy ending. To restore your own sense of peace, calm, and, yes, happiness, you need to stop fears from writing the script of your life.

Setting the Stage

In the play *As You Like It*, William Shakespeare wrote, "All the world's a stage, and all the men and women merely players: they have their exits and their entrances; and one man in his time plays many parts." Put another way—life is a drama. Sure, there are light moments, but most of us don't live within some sort of frivolous sitcom. Each of us is called to deal with serious issues and handle difficult situations. That's just the way it is.

For too long, you've allowed your anxieties to set the stage of everything that happens to you. For too long, you've allowed your fear to act as the director of your life, determining how you act and respond. For too long, the producer of this play that is your life has produced little relief from the unending concerns and stress. You've allowed yourself to be played, to be directed instead of insisting on taking charge yourself. You must decide to write your own script and set your own stage.

Ask yourself, when you wake up in the morning, whose script you are following, whose stage you are walking on to. Anxieties, fears, and worries set a dark and ominous stage with a script full of negatives. That doesn't have to be your life. You can refuse to play along.

Positive Point of View

Every story is told from a particular point of view. Each one of us has an attitude about life. We're either optimists or pessimists. We expect either good things to happen or bad things to happen. Now, you might say, aren't there people who expect neither good things nor bad things? What are they—optimists or pessimists? The absence of expecting good things isn't all that positive, so I would say those people are really not neutral; they are pessimists.

If you're anxiety-driven about something, you're a pessimist about it. The more things that cause you anxiety, the more pessimistic you are about your life. This is the script you've been operating from. It's time to fire those scriptwriters and take over yourself, switching from a negative, pessimistic worldview to a positive, optimistic one.

Talk It Out

One of the best ways I know to reorient your attitude is to have a heart-to-heart with yourself. Some people do this silently, inside their own minds, and others prefer to hold an audible conversation with themselves. One woman I worked with would argue with herself like an opposing attorney, talking to herself out loud. She said it helped to hear what she had to say out loud because she had an easier time detecting the emotions underlying the various arguments. If something didn't sound right, she'd stop and repeat the statement to herself, working through it until it made more sense. So she didn't disturb other family members, she'd often do this while taking a walk. Everyone just assumed she was on a cell phone.

Another woman I know would hold her conversations with herself in front of a mirror, looking herself directly in the eye. Other people, as I said, will have this conversation privately, in the confines of their own minds. How you do it isn't as important as that you do it. There is something valuable in articulation, in requiring yourself to produce the reasons behind what you do and then making those reasons visible and examinable. It's not unlike what people do with their therapists in what is known as talk therapy (as opposed to art therapy or music therapy). It's not unlike what people do when they talk with trusted friends, loved ones, or mentors. All these dialogues can be extremely useful, but you've got to learn how to have these conversations with yourself. Sometimes no one else is around or available, and you need to start building trust with yourself.

As you engage in this inner dialogue, don't forget what you learned in chapter 8 about controlling the volume. Pay attention to the volume of the negative and the positive. Be aware of when you need to change the dials and allow in more positives. This is especially true when problem-solving. You'll need to crank up optimism, hope, and joy so you can find the motivation and courage to find and implement a solution.

Write It Out

Some of you simply aren't verbal. If you aren't the type of person who processes things in an auditory way, I encourage you to articulate how you feel through writing. Many of the people I've worked with find great freedom of expression through journaling. This has an added benefit in that you have a written record of your inner discussions that you can review and refer back to. At the end of each chapter in this book, an anchoring activity has utilized this methodology. Those of you who are writers have done each one. Those of you who are talkers may have talked through your answers instead of writing them.

Some of you may already incorporate journaling into your daily or weekly habits. Journaling can be positive, negative, or neutral in helping you work through your anxieties. If you are merely chronicling the events of your day, like a daily calendar, this is probably going to be neutral. This can certainly be part of working through your anxieties, writing them down so you know what they are, but it falls short if that's all you do. Journaling can be negative if you use it to give full voice to your fears and concerns. Words are powerful, and by turning over your words to your worries, you strengthen them and weaken your resolve to take control of your life. While you need to articulate the truth of your anxieties and their consequences in your life, you also need to take control of that dialogue. You need to look for and record the positives in yourself, your life, and your expectations for each day, setting your own stage for optimism, hope, and joy to make a daily appearance.

The other day I was thinking about getting a new car. The one I've got isn't that old, but since I've had it, it's spent more time in my mechanic's garage than mine. I'm not sure I'd call it a lemon, but it's definitely citrusy. So I was looking online for possible transportation alternatives. I found a car I really liked and was amazed in the weeks that followed how many times I saw it. It was everywhere. I could hardly drive down the street without seeing one. The weird thing was I'd never really paid attention to that car before. As soon as it was in my sights, it's all I saw. You need to set your sights on the positive things in life, and if you do, you'll start to notice them everywhere.

Improvisation

I've heard that the best actors don't so much recite their lines as live them. These actors are so familiar with their character and the context of the surroundings in the play that their lines well up out of them as a natural consequence of living their character's life on stage. As a result, they won't always say the same lines the same way every performance. They live within their script and allow for inspiration and occasionally for improvisation. Some theater companies don't have scripts at all, just well-understood scenarios, and are known for improvising entire scenes.

I remember going to see a friend in a local play. It was an enjoyable experience, and I detected nothing wrong in the performance. After it was over, my friend apologized. He said one of the other actors had been late for an entrance, and he and the others on stage had to improvise until that actor finally showed up. I guess by my expression he could tell I hadn't been aware there was a problem, so he took me through the scene again, explaining the additions. They'd seemed so much a part of the flow of the play that I hadn't noticed. I remember thinking how impressed I was by their flexibility.

Sometimes that's what life is like. The script you write and the stage you set in the morning may change by midday, and you'll need to adjust and be flexible, all within the general feeling of the scene you've set up. When the unexpected happens, it doesn't have to trigger a storm of negativity. Instead, adjust your day and continue to move through it, keeping the same tone and attitude.

ANCHORING ACTIVITY

For this chapter, I'd like you to write a script for your life tomorrow or next week. Make it at least one day but not more than a week, so the assignment is short enough to accomplish but the concept is small enough to wrap your brain around. If even a single day seems too much to do, pick out a single scene from a day and work through a script for it. Before you start, there are several things you need to decide as you set the stage for your script:

- What sort of a character do you want to be? How do you want to be perceived by the other "players" on stage? Do you want to be considered frantic, chaotic, anxious, irritable, easily frustrated, or short-tempered? Or do you want to be seen as measured, relaxed, friendly, easygoing, and happy? Setting up your character will determine how you act toward each thing that happens to you, so it's important to consider who you want to be and act accordingly.

- What do you anticipate will happen to you? What are you expecting and how will you, as this character, react? Pay special attention to activities you have during the day that you currently consider negative. Maybe it's driving to work and you hate the traffic, so it always makes you irritated and nervous. How could you act instead? Can you determine beforehand that you're going to put in a special CD or tune into an oldies station and attempt to sing the lyrics to as many songs as you can? Can you determine beforehand that you're going to look for ways to be polite to other drivers and spread some positive actions on the road? Can you determine beforehand that you're going to pay attention to the drivers in the other cars and acknowledge each one as a person just trying to get to work instead of as a potential problem trying to mess up your commute? What's going to happen during the scenes in your day, and how are you going to act in each?

- How do you anticipate other people acting toward you? In any given day, you need to deal with yourself, with actions that happen, and with other people. These three make up the majority of our days. As you write your script, don't neglect to consider this third aspect. What you think other people think about you determines how you interpret their actions. If you think someone doesn't like you, an abruptly ended conversation is because she's mad at you instead of another incoming call. If you think someone is critical of your abilities, a positive comment about your work becomes a snide remark or a subtle jab. If you think someone is dismissive of you as a person, his failure to say hello is because he doesn't think you're worth acknowledging instead of because of his own stress and work level. Just as you can assign yourself the role of villain or victim, you can do the same thing with other people. Try to avoid this and write a script that reflects reality and is not based on negative perceptions. As often as it's possible to be positive, do so.

Fix in your mind the length of your play—is it a single scene, a day, or a week? The curtain rises and you introduce the main character—you. What are you like? What are your dominant characteristics?

Now, given these characteristics, describe what is going to happen and how your character is going to react to each situation.

As you move through the script, how are you going to relate to others? What can you say and do, within character, to interact as positively as possible with those around you?

Finally, what is the message of your script? What concepts, thoughts, and priorities are you trying to portray? Who do you want to be, and what do you want to emphasize?

There will come a time when being positive and taking control of your life will feel more natural and less like "acting." But again, it's all about baby steps. You need to start somewhere and begin to work up. You need to practice. Talk to yourself. Write down your thoughts and feelings. Become comfortable with the new, positive, more relaxed you and learn to improvise. Change is possible; I see it all the time. Is it generally slow? Yes. But only because by the time people decide they want or need to change, they want that change to happen immediately and their expectations are out of synch with reality. Slow and steady may not seem glamorous, but, as the fable says, it wins the race.

When I was growing up, I remember people talking about getting their "act" together. It meant they had made positive changes in their lives and were starting to live in a better way. This chapter has been about getting your "act" together, about making positive changes in your life and starting to live a better, happier, more content way. This chapter has been a lot about you—you writing your own script, you setting your own stage, you directing your own scene. And, ultimately, you are the one who has to do it. However, by now you should realize I never think this is something you have to do alone.

God's power and provision are always available to you. He is in your corner and would love to provide the background for your script through his presence and promises in Scripture. Psalm 18:20–24 in the *Message* says, "GOD made my life complete when I placed all the pieces before him. When I got my act together, he gave me a fresh start. Now I'm alert to GOD's ways; I don't take God for granted. Every day I review the way he works; I try not to miss a trick. I feel put back together, and I'm watching my step. GOD rewrote the text of my life when I opened the book of my heart to his eyes." As you're writing the script of your life each day, don't forget to review the way God works; try not to miss a trick. His desire is to rewrite the text of your life.

Father, show me your ways every day. When I wake up in the morning, dazzle the eyes of my heart with who you are and what you've promised for me. Help me to say, "This is the day the Lord has made; I will rejoice and be glad in it." Allow this joy to define my character today, tomorrow, and beyond.

15

Relief through Trust and Faith in God

Choose Where to Anchor

This final chapter is going to be a little different. Instead of an anchoring activity at the end, I want you to think of the entire chapter as an anchoring activity. I want you to commit to anchoring your life in the bedrock of God. You have been anchoring your life in the sandy shoals of your anxieties, worries, fears, and concerns. As a result, you've been tossed about by the waves of life, unanchored and often adrift. Your anxieties have been in charge, and you have not.

This mirrors what the apostle Paul talks about in Ephesians 4 when he speaks about the benefits of spiritual maturity or, you could say, the benefits of being spiritually anchored. He says, "Then we will no longer be infants, tossed back and forth by the waves, and blown here and there by every wind of teaching and by the cunning and craftiness of men in their deceitful scheming" (v. 14). If I've tried to do anything in this book, it is to help you see how much your anxieties consist of deceitful scheming. They are not based in reality, and they do not teach you the truth. They do not grant you freedom in your life; on the contrary, they enslave you. By clinging to them, you are not protecting or enhancing or guarding your life; you're conceding it, minute by minute, hour by hour, day by day, choice by choice. This is not the life God desires for you to live.

You have been placing your trust and faith in your own fears. When they speak, you listen intently and act accordingly. Even when faced with evidence to the contrary, your faith lies with them. When you trust in your fears, you doubt God. When you align yourself with your fears, you move yourself farther away from God. When you cling to your fears, you cling to your own perverted sense of control.

There is only one way to claim true control over your life: you have to surrender it. You've already been surrendering your life to the false reality of your fears; I implore you to surrender your life, instead, fully to God. Eugene Peterson in the *Message* puts the concept this way: getting down on your knees is the only way to get back on your feet (James 4:10).

Comfort Zone

I've said it before in several ways, but I want to say it again plainly: you have grown comfortable in your fears and anxieties. In a perverse way, they have become the known, the predictable, your comfort zone of behavior and expectation. To use a phrase from the book of Job, your anxieties and fears are "miserable comforts" but comforts still. You are more comfortable giving them control over your life than you are giving your life over to God. You've allowed your anxieties to provide you with meager, miserable comforts instead of claiming the true comfort promised by your loving Father. Listen to him argue passionately in his own defense in Isaiah 51:

211

I, even I, am he who comforts you.
  Who are you that you fear mortal men,
  the sons of men, who are but grass,
that you forget the LORD your Maker,
  who stretched out the heavens
  and laid the foundations of the earth,
that you live in constant terror every day
  because of the wrath of the oppressor,
  who is bent on destruction?
For where is the wrath of the oppressor?
  The cowering prisoners will soon be set free;
they will not die in their dungeon,
  nor will they lack bread.
For I am the LORD your God,
  who churns up the sea so that its waves roar—
  the LORD Almighty is his name.
I have put my words in your mouth
  and covered you with the shadow of my hand—
I who set the heavens in place,
  who laid the foundations of the earth,
  and who say to Zion, "You are my people." (vv. 12–16)

Do not take meager, miserable comfort any longer in your anxieties; choose to believe God when he says, "I, even I, am he who comforts you." He is stronger, more powerful, and mightier than the fears and anxieties that oppress you, no matter what lies those fears and anxieties tell you.

There is, of course, another part of this: you must allow yourself to be comforted by God; you must accept his comfort. To do this, you need to reject the tie—the relationship—you have with your anxieties. They've become so much a part of you that to reject them can seem tantamount to rejecting who you are. Again, in a perverse and paradoxical way, you've developed a relationship, a friendship, with your anxieties that must be broken. This friendship is not grounded in the spiritual realm, in God-reality, as it says in the *Message*; it is grounded firmly in the perceptions and deceptions, in the lies, of this world. Tying yourself to your anxieties ties you to this world.

To go with God, you have to give up these ties to the world, this relationship you have with your anxieties. James 4:4–10 clearly shows you can't have it both ways. The world and God are in direct competition with each other for your heart and mind. You already know what happens to your heart and mind when the world—when your anxieties and fears—are ascendant. Day by day, step by step, choice by choice, begin to shift your allegiance from the world of your anxieties, worries, and fears to God.

Accepting Yourself

Your relationship with your fears and anxieties damages and interferes with your relationship with God. It sabotages your relationships with other people. It also decimates another vital relationship: your relationship with self. Your fears and anxieties turn your own body and mind against you as you struggle to manage their devastating emotional terrors and debilitating physical assaults. They make you doubt yourself; they make you doubt your sanity; they make you doubt your health; they make you doubt your life. What you do is never enough. The steps you take are never sufficient. Again, these are the black-and-white false absolutes of your anxieties.

God, however, comes with a different set of absolutes where you are concerned:

- He loves you (Deut. 23:5).
- He says you are his precious child (1 John 3:1).
- He wants you to be with him always (John 3:16).
- He knows who you are and loves you still (Ps. 139:1).
- His love for you will never fail (1 Cor. 13:8).

- Nothing can snatch you from his hand (John 10:28–29).
- He does not want you to live in fear (Ps. 27:1).

God knows and accepts who you are. To change and grow as a person, you need to know and accept yourself. This puts you on the same page with God so together you can turn to the next page of your life—a page where fear is removed, a page where joy and peace are restored.

Grasping Grace

Anxieties scream that the worst that could happen will. They are firmly rooted in the negative, in the pessimistic. The world of worry is a glass that is perpetually not only half empty but draining out all the time. In such a world, there is little room or ability to perceive a concept as astonishingly optimistic and positive as grace.

I've heard the grace of God explained as unmerited favor. It's not something that can be earned; it is a divine gift. Grace operates in a world where the best that could possibly happen does. It is firmly rooted in the positive, in the optimistic. The world of grace is not the world of the empty glass; it is the world of a good measure, pressed down, shaken together and running over, poured into your lap (Luke 6:38). Grace is a world of amazing abundance that is given as a gift and not as a result of works (Rom. 11). You can't lose grace; you can only reject it.

As you continue to work through overcoming your fears, taming your anxieties, and deflating your worries, allow God—his love, his promises, and his grace—to fill up all those created vacancies. As you turn away from your relationship with your fears, turn toward a deeper and stronger relationship with God. Instead of filling your mind with the content of your concerns, fill it with the promises and passionate love of your heavenly Father.

I challenge you to get to know God better. Think of all the time, energy, and resources you have devoted to thinking about, worrying about, examining, and fighting against your anxieties and fears. Turn that time over to God, to getting to know him, to reading his Word, to prayer, to meditating on his character and divine nature. This is time well spent. This is productive, uplifting, renewing time. Become as intimately aware of the presence of God's Spirit in your life as you were of the presence of your anxieties. Allow the greatness of God to outshine those pale shadows.

Don't Give Up

The only way to ensure defeat is to give up, so don't. Changing from a life devoted to anxieties, pessimism, and distrust to a life devoted to optimism, hope, and joy takes time and effort. It is a journey, a journey from the dark into the light. This journey is a familiar one that began on the very first day. Genesis 1:5 says, "And there was evening, and there was morning—the first day." This divine progression from evening to morning, from darkness to light, was recently pointed out to me. The world says that a day begins in the morning and ends at night—that we go from light into darkness every day. I guess, from the world's point of view, that's appropriate. God, however, turns this around. His design moves things from darkness to light, so a day starts in the evening but ends in the morning. I like that. Your life of fear, of darkness, is designed by God to move to a life of hope, of light. So don't give up when things seem dark; you just haven't reached God's promised dawn yet. Keep moving, keep hoping, keep believing, keep choosing to trust and put your faith in God. As you do, you'll begin to notice your world lightening around the edges with the emergence of a glorious morning.

God is really good with glorious mornings. Think of a particular morning in the city of Jerusalem two thousand years ago.

A woman named Mary went to a tomb, fully prepared to tend to a broken and lifeless body. God, however, had something else in the works. God, through his power, turned that death into life. What was deemed unstoppable, inevitable, an absolute fact of death, turned out not to be so. The black-and-white thinking of the world was proven wrong, again. The naysayers were wrong; the faithful were right. God is faithful. Be faithful yourself and keep allowing him to transform your doubts into faith, your fears into an opportunity to trust.

Listen to God more than your fears. Keep turning down their volume every chance you get and turn up the voice of God. As I told you before, real change is possible; I see it all the time. I guess that's another way of saying I see God all the time. He's working in my life. I see him working in the lives of others. And I have faith he is able to work in yours.

Notes

Introduction

1. http://www.merriam-webster.com/dictionary/anxiety.

Chapter 1

1. National Institutes of Health, NIH Publication no. 09-3879, "Anxiety Disorders" (2009): 1.

2. National Institutes of Health, NIH Publication no. 07-4677, "When Worry Gets Out of Control: Generalized Anxiety Disorder" (2007): 2.

3. National Institutes of Health, NIH Publication no. 09-3879, "Anxiety Disorders" (2009): 13.

4. Ibid., 4.

5. Ibid.

6. Ibid., 11.

7. Ibid., 10.

8. http://www.nlm.nih.gov/medlineplus/obsessivecompulsivedisorder.html.

Chapter 4

1. http://www.cancer.gov/dictionary/?CdrID=457951.

2. http://www.drugabuse.gov/Infofacts/marijuana.html.

3. http://www.ncbi.nlm.nih.gov/pubmed/11066185.

Chapter 6

1. http://www.nimh.nih.gov/health/topics/depression/men-and-depression /signs-and-symptoms-of-depression/index.shtml.

2. "Co-Occurring Anxiety Complicates Treatment Response for Those with Major Depression," NIMH Science Update, February 25, 2008, http://www.nimh.nih.gov/science-news/2008/co-occurring-anxiety-complicates-treatment-response-for-those-with-major-depression.shtml.

3. Ibid.

Chapter 8

1. http://www.merriam-webster.com/dictionary/objective.

2. http://www.merriam-webster.com/dictionary/subjective.

Chapter 13

1. http://nimh.nih.gov/health/publications/anxiety-disorders/treatment-of-anxiety-disorders.shtml.

Gregory L. Jantz, PhD, is a popular speaker and award-winning author. He is a licensed mental health counselor and a certified chemical dependency professional. Dr. Jantz is the founder of The Center for Counseling and Health Resources, Inc., a leading mental health and chemical dependency health-care facility known as "a place of hope."

The Center for Counseling and Health Resources, Inc., is a whole-person treatment center. Individuals from across the United States as well as the rest of the world come to participate in the hope-filled work of recovery from a range of traumas and addictive behaviors. Dr. Jantz's whole-person approach addresses the emotional, relational, intellectual, physical, and spiritual dimensions of each person with a unique, tailored treatment plan.

His compassionate, solution-oriented viewpoints on timely topics, plus a natural gift for storytelling, make him a sought-after guest on local and national radio and television. He speaks nationally at conferences, seminars, and retreats on a wide variety of topics, utilizing his extensive expertise and experience.

Dr. Jantz has been married for twenty-eight years to his wife, LaFon. They have two sons, Gregg and Benjamin.

Ann McMurray is a freelance writer living in Brier, Washington, whose partnership with Dr. Jantz goes back many years.

For more information about the work of the Center, please call the Center's toll-free number: 888-771-5166. You can also contact the

Center through its website at www.aplaceofhope.com or by mail at P.O. Box 700, Edmonds, WA 98020.

Other Resources by Dr. Gregory Jantz

God Can Help You Heal
Happy for the Rest of Your Life
Healing the Scars of Emotional Abuse
Healthy Habits, Happy Kids: A Practical Plan to Help Your Family
Hope, Help, and Healing for Eating Disorders
Moving beyond Depression: A Whole-Person Approach to Healing
The Body God Designed: How to Love the Body You've Got While You Get the Body You Want
The Molding of a Champion: Helping Your Child Shape a Winning Destiny
The Total Temple Makeover: How to Turn Your Body into a Temple You Can Rejoice In
Thin Over 40: The Simple 12-Week Plan
Too Close to the Flame: Recognizing and Avoiding Sexualized Relationships
Turning the Tables on Gambling: Hope and Help for an Addictive Behavior

Hope and Healing for the Victims of Emotional Abuse

Gregory L. Jantz, PhD

with Ann McMurray

Healing the Scars of Emotional Abuse

Revised and Updated

Revell
a division of Baker Publishing Group
www.RevellBooks.com

Available at your local bookstore.

A Practical and Inspiring Resource for Women on Managing Anger

Every Woman's Guide *to* **Managing Your Anger**

Gregory L. Jantz, PhD

with Ann McMurray

Ω Revell
a division of Baker Publishing Group
www.RevellBooks.com

Available at your local bookstore.